American Art Association

Catalog of the Private Collection of Modern Paintings

Belonging to Mr. William H. Shaw

American Art Association

Catalog of the Private Collection of Modern Paintings
Belonging to Mr. William H. Shaw

ISBN/EAN: 9783744657358

Printed in Europe, USA, Canada, Australia, Japan

Cover: Foto ©Thomas Meinert / pixelio.de

More available books at **www.hansebooks.com**

CATALOGUE

OF THE

PRIVATE COLLECTION

OF

MODERN PAINTINGS

BELONGING TO

MR. WILLIAM H. SHAW

OF THIS CITY

TO BE ABSOLUTELY SOLD BY AUCTION

ON

FRIDAY EVENING, MARCH 7TH

AT 7.30 O'CLOCK

AT THE AMERICAN ART GALLERIES

6 EAST 23D STREET (MADISON SQUARE)

WHERE THE PAINTINGS ARE NOW ON EXHIBITION
DAY AND EVENING, SUNDAYS EXCEPTED

THOMAS E. KIRBY, AUCTIONEER

AMERICAN ART ASSOCIATION, MANAGERS

NEW YORK
1890

CONDITIONS OF SALE.

1. The highest bidder to be the Buyer, and if any dispute arise between two or more Bidders, the Lot so in dispute shall be immediately put up again and re-sold.

2. The Purchasers to give their names and addresses, and to pay down a cash deposit, or the whole of the Purchase-money, *if required*, in default of which the Lot or Lots so purchased to be immediately put up again and re-sold.

3. The Lots to be taken away at the Buyer's expense and Risk on the morning following each session of the Sale, between 9 and 12 o'clock, and the remainder of the Purchase-money to be absolutely paid, or otherwise settled for to the satisfaction of the Auctioneer, on or before delivery; in default of which the undersigned will not hold himself responsible if the Lots be lost, stolen, damaged, or destroyed, but they will be left at the sole risk of the Purchaser.

4. The sale of any painting is not to be set aside on account of any error in the description. All are exposed for Public Exhibition one or more days, and are sold just as they are without recourse.

5. To prevent inaccuracy in delivery and inconvenience in the settlement of the purchases, no Lot can, on any account, be removed during the Sale.

6. Upon failure to comply with the above conditions, the money deposited in part payment shall be forfeited; all Lots uncleared within the time aforesaid shall be re-sold by public or private Sale, without further notice, and the deficiency (if any) attending such re-sale, shall be made good by the defaulter at this Sale, together with all charges attending the same. This Condition is without prejudice to the right of the Auctioneer to enforce the contract made at this Sale, without such re-sale, if he thinks fit.

THOMAS E. KIRBY, AUCTIONEER.

ARTISTS REPRESENTED.

Beauquesne (4),
Berne-Bellecour,
Béraud,
Beyle,
Binet,
Blum,
Bridgman,
Brooks,
Brown, J. G.,
Brown, W. M.,

Charpin,
Chilminski,
Col,
Croegaerdt,

De Neuville,
Detti,
Diaque,
Dupré,

Feron,
Frappa,

Gardanné (2),
Gifford, S. R.,
Groux,
Guillemet,
Guzzardi,

Hagborg,
Haquette,
Harnett,
Hart, James M.,
Hart, William,
Henner,
Hyon,

Jacque,
Johnson, David,

Kray,

Magnus,
Massini,

McCord,
Meissner,
Meyer von Bremen,
Miralles,
Moormanc,
Morelli,
Mouchot,
Musin,

Pellefigue,
Phelan,
Pinchart,

Quartley,

Rau,
Ream,
Ricci,
Rota,
Roumégous (2),
Rousseau, Theo.,

Salmson,
Sani,
Schenck,
Schmutzler,
Schuchard,
Seifert,
Sell,
Smith, H. P. (2),
Soulacroix,
Suterl,

Tamburini,
Tortez,

Ulrich,

Van den Bos,
Verboeckhoeven,
Vernon,

Walker,
Witt,

Zuber Buhler.

CATALOGUE.

COLLECTION OF

WILLIAM H. SHAW.

TO BE SOLD IN THE FOLLOWING ORDER

On FRIDAY EVENING, MARCH 7th, at 8 o'clock

₊ DIMENSIONS ARE GIVEN IN INCHES, AND REFER TO CANVAS OR PANEL, EXCLUSIVE OF FRAME. THE FIRST FIGURES INDICATE THE HEIGHT, THE SECOND THE WIDTH.

No. 136
CHRISTIAN SELL (Deceased)

Born in Altona, Denmark, 1831. Studied at Düsseldorf Academy. Member Royal Academy, Düsseldorf.

" The Picket Guard"
8 x 10

'' Sell has made the life of the German soldier a part of himself. His study of it has been mechanically faithful. He is the leading painter of military *genre* in Germany. He has essayed grander subjects, as witness the 'Battle of Königgrätz,' in the Berlin National Gallery, and his pictures of the Thirty-Years' War are full of life and character.''—FRIEDERICH PECHT.

Professor Sell's pictures are characterized by their purity of color, excellence of drawing, and fine finish. He prefers the cabinet size for them, and rarely exceeds it. He bases his work on careful sketches and studies, and is noted for the methodical accuracy with which his details are presented. To the German army he is what Detaille is to the French, a faithful registrar not only of the events of life in barrack, camp, and field, but also a reliable authority on points of costume and armament. While he lacks some of the freedom of execution of his French contemporary, he excels him in the completeness of his finish, and in the fine local character which he invariably gives to the surroundings of his groups, of which " The Picket Guard " is a worthy example.

No. 137

LEON VICTOR DUPRÉ (deceased)

Born at Limoges, 1816.   *Brother and pupil of Jules Dupré.*
Medals at Paris, 1849, *and Philadelphia,* 1876.

"Landscape"

12 x 16

" It is the inevitable vocation, in the history of families, of the
greater talent to obscure the lesser. The name of Jules Dupré is a
household word with art lovers. Who recalls that of Leon Victor
Dupré? And yet we have here a very respectable talent, which
but for its subjection to a more commanding genius might have
made an individual place for itself."—LOUIS ENAULT.

It was at once the fortune and the misfortune of Victor Dupré that he was
the brother of a great artist. Still worse, he was his pupil. Four years
younger than Jules Dupré, Victor early exhibited artistic capacities of a high
order of promise. He entered upon a course of study in his brother's studio, and
the influence of his master attaches itself to all of his works. One traces in them
the ideas and the principles of Jules Dupré, even when Victor is most desirous
to assert his own individuality. Nevertheless he won honors at home and
abroad, and his pictures found a ready acceptance with amateurs, which they
still enjoy. They possess pleasing color, forcibly applied, and are frequently
characterized by sparkling brilliancy of effect. Victor Dupré preceded his
famous brother to the grave by more than a decade, and in the greater fame of
that brother his own memory has been relegated to undeserved neglect.

No. 138

LOUIS ERNEST GROUX.................Paris

" The Coquette "

12 x 8

" This pirate bold upon love's sea
   Will let no passing heart go free ;
      No barque by these bright eyes espied
      May sail away o'er life's blue tide
   Till all its treasures yielded be.

Her craft, the *Conquest*, waits for thee
   Where her swift rapine none may see ;
      From shadowing coves on thee will glide
      This pirate bold."

—SAMUEL WADDINGTON.

A coquetry reinforced by such beauty as this should be, indeed, formidable to the susceptible among the ruder sex. The victims of M. Groux's coquette can, however, find satisfaction, like the defeated Roman soldier, in the fact that they have succumbed to an enemy who could not be resisted. It is a charming head, full of expression, of what the French call *esprit*, and with those clean-cut contours that constitute the highest type of feminine beauty, painted, as are indeed all these feminine types in which the artist rejoices, with a purity and freshness of color and a fluency and delicacy of touch in keeping with the subject.

No. 139

N. A. BROOKS.........................New York

"Still Life"

14 x 18

" The range of the painter of still life being narrow, he must rely on executive perfection for success. There can be no middle ground between a good still life picture and a poor one. We have a great many painters of the latter grade. Prominent among the former is N. A. Brooks, to whom one can always look for good grouping, good color and tone, and a representation of form and textures in keeping with the rest."—*The Collector*, 1889.

A book, a jar, a teapot; the casual grouping of familiar objects on a table furnishes the artist an excuse for the display of his powers of imitation. The rest depends upon himself. His drawing must have the accuracy of a photograph. His brush must possess the faculty of reproducing natural tints and surfaces like a mirror. When he can command these forces, as Mr. Brooks does, he is not a mere mechanical copyist of facts, but a producer of pictures whose attractiveness will never cease to entitle them to a place upon the collector's walls.

No. 140

SANDFORD R. GIFFORD, N.A. (deceased)

*Born in Saratoga County, N. Y. Studied with John R. Smith,
New York. Elected a member of the National Academy, New
York, 1854. Commended for excellence in landscape painting
at the Centennial Exposition, Philadelphia, 1876. Died, 1880.*

" Landscape "

12 X 20

" When the long nights return, and find us met
    Where he was wont to meet us, and the flame
    Of the deep hearth-stone gladdens as of old,
    And there is cheer, as ever in that place,
    How shall our utmost nearing close the gap,
    Known, but till then scarce measured ? Or what light
    Of cheer for us, his gracious presence gone,
    His speech delayed, till none shall fail to miss
    That halting voice, yet sure ; speaking, it seemed,
    The one apt word ? For well the painter knew
    Art's alchemy and law ; her nobleness
    Was in his soul, her wisdom in his speech.
    And loyalty was housed in that true heart.
    Gentle, yet strong, and yielding not one whit
    Of right or purpose. Now, not more afar
    The light of last year's Yule fire than the smile
    Of Gifford, nor more irreclaimable
    Its vapor mingled with the wintry air."

           —EDMUND C. STEDMAN : *" Gifford."*

These touching lines, which Mr. Stedman indited upon the death of the artist, index the personal esteem in which he was held. In his artistic connections much the same sentiment prevailed. He represented a transition period in our art—a passing away of the old, and a building up of the new—and the sincerity and dignity with which he labored in the path he believed the right one compelled the respect even of those who disagreed with his beliefs. His genius is aptly summed up by Professor Weir, in his official report of the fine arts at the Centennial Exhibition of 1876 : " This artist is varied in his powers, and sustained, free, and finished in his methods. His pictures always manifest great elevation of thought and feeling. They are the interpretation of the profounder sentiments of Nature rather than of her superficial aspects."

No. 141

WILFRED C. BEAUQUESNE

Born at Rennes. Pupil of Vernet and of Lecomte.

" Stragglers "

25 x 19

" Stragglers are the ghosts of the army. They follow in its wake like shadows. Physical weakness, weariness, or indolence may be the cause of their defection from the ranks. Accident may separate them from their companies. They incur personal perils unknown to soldiers marching in bodies, and their experiences are full of the romance of hair-breadth escapes."—HARRISON : *" Diary of a War Tramp."*

Two soldiers, belonging to different commands, as their uniforms show, have met upon a common footing as stragglers, and joined company. Guided by the broad trail left by the army in its advance, they follow in its wake. Their track lies through a desolate country, rendered doubly forlorn by the ravages of war. It is invested with unknown perils. Their progress is stayed by the discovery, far in advance, of masses of troops, whose identity the distance renders it impossible to fix. Are they friends or foes? The question is a momentous one, and the wanderers slacken the speed of their steps to discuss it. Painted in the artist's best manner, this picture is excellent in color, in characterization, and in the simple story it tells in direct terms.

No. 142

GEORGES CROEGAERDT................. .Paris

Born at Antwerp, Belgium.   Pupil of Van Beers.

" Maidenhood "

10 x 8

" Maiden ! with the meek brown eyes,
    In whose orbs a shadow lies
    Like the dusk in evening skies !

" Standing with reluctant feet,
    Where the brook and river meet,
    Womanhood and childhood fleet ! "
                —HENRY WADSWORTH LONGFELLOW.

Croegaerdt has acquired from his master Van Beers some of the latter's extraordinary dexterity in seizing upon the traits of feminine character, and transferring them to canvas. He aspires, however, less to the dashing and sensational types that Van Beers has made his own. His most successful idealizations of womanhood have been marked by delicacy of feeling and truth of sentiment, and he has been exceptionally felicitous in his renditions of young womanhood at that adolescent period when, as in this example, the living original possesses those subtleties of beauty and expression that are most difficult for the painter to realize. His Salon exhibits, which in 1888 and 1889 won Croegaerdt high commendation, are of a more ambitious character of composition, painted with decided freedom and force.

No. 143

LOUIS BÉRAUD............................Paris

Born at Lyons. Pupil of Savastre and Bonnat. Medal, 1883, Hors concours.

"A Corner of the Studio"

22 X 26

"Béroud, who with the aspirations of an artist was compelled at the very commencement of his career to face the stern realities of war, is an anomaly among Frenchmen. Although he served in the National Guard during the siege of Paris, and experienced all the hurly-burly and horrors of the Commune, he has never painted a military picture. Scenes of peace, and of peace associated with artistic surroundings, are his forte ; vast interiors, with walls crowded with pictures and ceilings made sumptuous with carvings and decorations, he paints with a master hand, animating them with groups of figures full of character and life. Such pictures other than these that he paints are masterly studies, ripe and strong in color, fine in tone, and replete with the sentiment that comes to an artist out of complete absorption in his work."—ALBERT WOLFF.

The tendency of Béroud to large decorative compositions is readily explained by the fact that his earlier art life was spent as a decorator. He has, however, produced some charming canvases of a less ambitious order, commonly pages of the daily life of the studio, a model in repose, a visitor inspecting a picture, a pupil—always, by preference, of the fair sex—seated at the easel, palette in hand. He dwells upon these efforts with a loving and lingering care, and speaks of them as his children. His larger works he calls his masters, because, in his opinion, he can never quite carry them to the point which his exacting self-criticism has made the standard.

No. 144

E. GALLARD LEPINAY....................Paris

Born in Spain.   Studied in Paris under Ziem.

"On the Mediterranean Sea"

26 x 38

"A wet sheet and a flowing sea,
   A wind that follows fast,
And fills the white and rustling sail,
   And bends the gallant mast ;
And white waves heaving high, my boys,
   The good ship tight and free—
The world of waters is our home,
   And merry men are we."

—ALLAN CUNNINGHAM.

The Mediterranean is a sea by itself. It enjoys a climate, an atmosphere and weather of its own. Its waters have a color one finds nowhere but here, its tides are swayed by caprices unknown in other seas, and its individual character has gained for it with mariners a place apart. M. Lepinay, who from the studio of Ziem long since stepped into a reputation of his own, has done with his brush for the Mediterranean much the same service as his master has performed for the Adriatic. He has largely devoted himself to scenes on the French and Spanish coast, which he paints with great animation, truth of local color and technical dash and spirit, rendering the brisk and sparkling movement of the water, the character and action of the shipping, and the picturesque variations of the coast-line with much fidelity and force.

No. 145

GEORGES PIERRE MARIÈ VAN DEN BOS..Paris

Born at Ghent, Belgium. · *Pupil of Lefebvre.*

"Among the Apple Blossoms"

Job

38 x 25

"Van den Bos belongs to the advanced modern type of Belgian,
to whom the world does not end at the Flemish frontiers. In art he
is more of a Parisian, both in thought and expression. Moreover,
he is one of those far from common spirits to whom it has been
permitted to read that marvellous riddle, the Parisienne's heart."—
PIERRE PAUL LEVY.

It is two of the painter's Parisiennes whom we see in this picture, *chic* and
coquettish daughters of the town, who have celebrated the advent of spring
with an excursion into the suburbs. You may be sure there is a comfortable
inn somewhere not too far away for high-heeled boots to reach it in comfort,
and agreeable company of the sex which carries the purse to preside at the
feast. This little invasion of the blossoming orchard has been a mere whim, a
tribute of capricious respect to nature which means nothing but a bit of gossip
by the way and a handful of wild blossoms in the centre of the dinner-table,
where they will wither in neglect before the *pousse-café* has been set upon the
board and mine host been called upon to produce that bill which is the one
inevitable penalty of every social festival. M. Van den Bos was the recipient
of an Honorable Mention at the Salon of 1889.

No. 146

MORSTON REAM......................New York.

Born in 1840. Devoted to painting cabinet pieces of fruit. Also known as a connoisseur and collector of pictures for purposes of trade.

"Fruit and Wine"

12 X 14

" It is an amiable talent, that of Ream's. It leaves on our walls pleasant reminders of modest repasts, represented with clear color and a delicate finish."— *The Arcadian.*

A composition of a sort familiar with this artist, displaying his usual careful execution, and light and agreeable scheme of color. The tints of oranges and grapes make a harmonious contrast, and the glass, partially filled with wine, is skilfully painted. The painter, an excellent judge of pictures, and thoroughly in sympathy with good art, was one of the apostles of American art in the present generation, and it is due to his influence that many representative works of native origin found their reception in private collections. His own pictures are widely popular, and, extensively distributed in the public exhibitions, have secured acceptance among collectors throughout the country.

No. 147

PIO RICCI.

Born at Arezzo, Italy, 1844. Pupil of Sienna Academy.

210

"A Difficult Choice"

18 x 14

" He has carried the painting of textures to a high degree of perfection. His patrician women of the Renaissance period, attractive in the picturesqueness and splendid in the sumptuousness of their dress, are especially satisfactory, and it is when he paints them in the magnificent palace interiors of the time that we see him at his best."—ALESSANDRO MORELLI.

Beauty at her jewel casket finds herself in a quandary not uncommon with her sex, in times remote or present. What jewels shall be found most appropriate with this crimson robe faced with blue is a question not lightly answered. Pearls are too pale. The flash of diamonds would disturb the rich harmony of her attire. Rubies? But their color does not match. And so the contents of the casket are tumbled about by an impatient hand and the choice of the necklace is, apparently, as far off as ever. The artist has made the settings of his scene appropriate to the subject. The accessories are as ornate and rich as their mistress is magnificent in her aristocratic presence. The gems whose conflicting claims to favor confuse her should, to be in keeping with the rest, represent the ransom of a principality at least.

2

No. 148

VICTOR TORTEZ ....Paris

Born at Paris.   Pupil of Gérôme and Stenner.

"Just from the Garden"

16 x 18

> "She will bring thee, all together,
> All delights of summer weather ;
> All the buds and bells of May,
> From dewy sward or thorny spray.
> Thou shalt, at one glance, behold
> The daisy and the marigold,
> White plumed lilies, and the first
> Hedge-grown primrose that has burst."
>
> —JOHN KEATS.

Flowers and sentiment go together. Certain poets have held that the colors of the floral kingdom have a meaning, and their perfumes an individual eloquence. That flowers have a language of their own we are aware, at least upon the authority of tradition. The maiden of M. Tortez's picture has evidently mastered this mystic tongue, and is communing with the trophies of her raid upon the garden in close confidence. We may be privileged to guess at the secrets she whispers to them, and to guess only. The painter's power of suggestion ceases there. But he has given us a picture full of nature, bright, airy and refreshing to the eye, with a freedom of touch with which the simplicity of the subject goes hand in hand.

No. 149

WILFRED C. BEAUQUESNE...............Paris

Born at Rennes. Pupil of Vernet and of Lecomte.

"Water in the Desert"

130

17 X 11

"One of the privations of the campaign was want of water. Wells were few and far between, and the water in them commonly bad. The natives, as they retreated before our advance, destroyed most of the cisterns. When the men discovered one of these tanks still intact it was an event indeed, and the excitement attendant on the discovery did not die away until canteens and soldiers were full of the grateful liquid, and the cistern as dry and empty as the troops had been before."—"*Campaigning in Algiers.*"

A portion of the army, advancing through the desert, panting and parched with thirst under the African sun, has reached the solitary and abandoned habitation of some Algerine who has fled before the invaders' approach. The leaders of the advance have found, in the wall surrounding the garden, the waste-pipe of the cistern, trickling moisture into the arid sand. It is a moment of joyous suspension of discipline. One soldier drinks his fill at the pipe. Another calls up the troop with a significant wave of his canteen. Ranks are broken, and while there is a drop in the cistern the progress of invasion is halted, and the invader forgets a future of battles in a present of refreshment all the more agreeable for its unexpectedness.

No. 150

A. SANI...Florence

"A New Treasure"

14 X 12

" Collectorship is a mild fôrm of insanity, but it is an amiable and harmless mania. I am most interested in those elderly gentlemen who gather up unconsidered trifles of bric-à-brac, from any hole or corner in which they can find it. Where do they put their treasures ? What do they do with them ? And what becomes of them when the collector in due course of nature can collect no more ? This is the mystery about my friends of the second-hand shops and the auction rooms that fascinates me and holds me as by a spell."— CHARLES LEVER.

One of Lever's amiable and harmless madmen has just added a treasure to his collection. He has secured his prize at a bargain, in his own estimation at least, and conveyed it safely home. Now, in the seclusion of his own chamber, he may revel in its beauties, which will grow no less, in his eyes, through continuous contemplation of them. It is one peculiarity of the inveterate collector that his last find is always his greatest. From the expression of Sani's self-satisfied old gentleman, it is manifest that he views his precious group as the central gem of all his jewels of rarity and ripe old age.

No. 151

AUGUSTIN FRANÇOIS ROUMÉGOUX......Paris

Born at Revel, France, 1851. Pupil of Cabanel.

"The Flax Breakers"

40 X 33

300

" In stony court-yards rings the axe's clang
Where once the troubadour his ballad sang,
And empty windows, staring at the sky,
Invite the vagrant bird that passes by ;
From the great fireplace rises no warm smoke,
And echo bears the dull and heavy stroke
Of the flax-breakers, who to their task bend
From early morn until the long day's end.
One glory only in these ruins abides,
But it atones for many wants besides ;
Beautiful still, as flowers amid decay,
The maids of Provence go their cheerful way."

—FRÉDÉRIC MISTRAL.

The painter has gone to his own country for a subject in this picture. The scene is in the spacious court-yard of one of those great farm-houses of the South of France that were, perhaps, once castles, and that preserve their solidity and strength in defiance of the waste and ravages of time. In the foreground, a stalwart peasant woman is breaking flax at a primitive contrivance almost as old as flax itself. A girl in the ripe beauty of young womanhood stands ready to supply her with fresh material for her use. In the rear of the courtyard a peasant, who has been chopping firewood, rests his axe upon the billet at his feet to wipe his streaming brow. M. Roumégoux gives us, in this picture, a graphic glimpse of the Provence of to-day of which his poet compatriot sings so eloquently in his famous verses.

No. 152

A. SUTERI

" Economy "

14 X 10

"Another of those Italians who go to the monastery for their subjects. This one, however, views the friar with a domestic rather
than a satirical or reverential eye. He paints him at his daily avoca-
tions, always good-naturedly, with good color and an eye for pictorial effect."—*Journal Pittoresque*, 1887.

In the convent cellar the cellarer, with a frugal bent of mind, is emptying
the lees of wine from casks and bottles into a bowl. He is draining the contents of a barrel into this receptacle. Flasks already emptied and a large jar
to receive the contents of the bowl offer further attestations to his economical
industry. What is no longer good wine, says his smiling face, may be very
good vinegar. The vaulted cellar loses itself in dusky ramifications, but the
figure of the cellarer is brightly lighted from an unseen window. The color is
cheerful and the contrast of light and shade brilliant in effect.

No. 153

GEORGES HYON.....................   Paris

Born at Paris.   Pupil of Protais.

'The Dog of the Regiment'

18 x 25

" Hyon, a pupil of Protais, who has also, we believe, enjoyed the instruction of Detaille, exhibited in the 1887 Salon a striking canvas, 'After Jena.' In 1888 he followed it with a still more imposing work, 'Waterloo,' based on a passage of Thiers' history. This year (1879) he sends an episode of the bloody 30th of August, 1870—'A Day of Battle : Beaumont.' Hyon won his spurs a decade ago. It is in these recent exhibitions, however, that he has shown himself at his strongest and best."—PAUL MARITZ.

The regiment is encamped during the annual manœuvres. A group of cronies from the ranks are taking their ease with the dog of the regiment for company. The dog of war, it may be added, is now an inseparable part of the French army. Every regiment has such a canine attachment. Often single companies have dogs of their own, and many of these sagacious brutes are trained to extraordinary feats of intelligence as bearers of messages and sentries with the outposts. M. Hyon's dog is, just now, engaged in the serious duty of begging a share of a human comrade's lunch, and although the latter shows no marked signs of an intention to yield a share of his bread and cheese, the suppliant, we may make safe to say, will not go hungry for long.

No. 154

FRANÇOIS MUSIN...... ....Brussels

*Born at Ostend. Studied at Antwerp and Brussels. Knight
of the Order of Leopold. Medals at London, Vienna,
Amsterdam.*

"A Fresh Breeze in the English Channel"

18 x 30

" The refluent ocean
Fled away from the shore and left the line of the sand beach
Covered with waifs of the tide, with kelp and the slippery sea-weed.
Back to its nethermost caves retreated the bellowing ocean,
Dragging adown the beach the rattling pebbles, and leaving
Inland and far up the shore the stranded boats of the sailors."

—HENRY WADSWORTH LONGFELLOW.

Born within sight and sound of the narrow sea which washes the coast of
the Netherlands, M. Musin, in the earliest stages of his art, turned naturally
to it for his subjects. He has roved the Flemish and Dutch coasts in quest of
pictures, and the productions of his easel provide the landmarks by which his
wanderings may be traced. It is with the shore and waters of his own
country that he is most at home, however, and he has made a close study of
their picturesque aspects and of the phenomena of the atmosphere that aid in
giving them interest. The boats of the fishermen and the luggers of the
traders, rocking on the long swells, buffeted by gales, lost in the fog banks or
left stranded on the shore by the outgoing tide, furnish him with material
abundant and varied enough to constitute a constant succession of pictures,
ever novel and fresh in character, and never lacking in interest. The subject
of " A Fresh Breeze " is found on the Flemish coast, near Ostend, where,
under pressure of wind and tide, a restless and turbulent sea is far commoner
than periods of placidity and calm.

No. 155

ALFRED SEIFERT...................Munich

Born in Horowitz, Bohemia, 1850. Pupil of Lindenschmidt.

"A Good Story"

12 X 14

"Seifert came before the public with compositions of an ambitious character, mainly historical, which, while good from an academic standpoint, were too cold and formal to arouse enthusiasm. Since he has descended to less ambitious themes he shows as an artist of much merit, and has enjoyed a success which he fully deserves."—
FRIEDRICH PECHT.

A worldly visitor has invaded the monastery. He has come on business, no doubt, for he has the look of a lawyer, and even the Church is not beyond the need of legal advice in these degenerate and contentious days. His entertainment has been hospitable. The ripest vintage of the convent casks has been brought up for his refreshment. His business concluded, the claims of sociability are allowed, and the news of the world, which only by accident invades this retreat of the unworldly, comes up for discussion. He carries some of it by him in print, and as he culls from the pages the details of some tale just piquant enough to be permissible in pious company, his hosts find themselves amply compensated for their hospitality. The quiet enjoyment of the story by the reader himself is discounted by the hearty merriment it arouses in his hosts as it approaches a climax which will certainly necessitate another drain on the resources of the wine vault.

No. 156

G. ROTA.................. ....Venice

"A Girl of To-Day"

18 x 14

"A girl of fullest heart she was;
Her spirit's lovely flame
Nor dazzled nor surprised, because
It always burned the same."
    —COVENTRY PATMORE.

The modern young woman, in spite of more or less philosophical and meta-physical dissections and detractions, is conceded, by right-minded persons, to be the highest type of the young girl that civilization has produced. To the simpler virtues of a ruder ancestral stock she adds the polish and refinement of our own time. Her elegance, her style and grace of carriage, her intelligence and culture, belong to the present. Her self-respect, her power to sustain her position and assert her dignity when occasion arises, are a heritage from the past. Her detractors have adopted the exceptions which the imperfections of human nature render inevitable as the rule, but the true girl of to-day affords a prompt and conclusive refutation of their imputations upon her. She is, as Rota paints her with the brush, and as the English poet presented her with the pen, a creation of whom we may well be proud, and to whom the future will render the just appreciation she deserves.

No. 157

A. TAMBURINI...........................Rome

Pupil of Ciceri. Medal, Academy of Fine Arts, Florence.

"A Little Worldly"

120

12 X 10

"They say that even the friar in his cell
　　Sometimes gives way to thoughts of vanity :
　Envies their lives who in the world do dwell,
　　And pines at heart for more variety :
　Bewigs his tonsure and discards his gown,
　And in his mind goes ruffling through the town."

—LORD BYRON.

Modern art has produced what might almost be called a distinct school—that of the painters of monks and of monastery pictures. In Italy, France, Germany, and England, painters have grown into fame upon the satire, humor, or purely narrative character of their representations of the life of the religious recluse. Some paint him with stinging satire, and others with sly humor that is full of disrespect for his cloth. Some see in him but the incarnation of a self-indulgent man, retired from the world out of sheer laziness and avoidance of its responsibilities, while others view him as the ascetic mortifying his flesh that his spirit may be chastened, and putting his body to penance to purify his soul. Tamburini takes the lighter view of the subject ; the Byronic view, without the Byronic irony and bitterness. The worldly thoughts aroused in his old friar's mind by a contemplation of the globe are evidently flavored with curiosity rather than intrigue, and do no violence to his vows and vocation.

No. 158

E. SALMSON...............................Paris

Born at Albert, France.   Pupil of Cogniet and of Bouguereau.

"The Fisherman's Daughter"

26 x 18

"Mlle. E. Salanson is one of the women of the present Salon. She treats subjects of the sea-coast with a frank and sympathetic touch.   Her 'Driftwood Gatherer' is a poem in itself, and her 'Fisherman's Daughter' a type whose acquaintanceship we can envy her.   To predict a future for a talent healthy and active would be assuming no merit of prophecy, since it affords its own prediction and guarantee in its works."—RENÉ MAIZEROY :   "*Le Salon de* 1885."

The commendation extended by the French critic to one of the two exhibits made by Mlle. Salanson in the exhibition noted received the substantial indorsement of the public, and the equally flattering, if less profitable substantiation of the press.   Restricting herself almost entirely to the class of subjects with which she won her first successes, she has varied them occasionally with portraiture, and has added annually to her reputation and popularity.   In 1886 her "Avant la Pêche," a fisher-girl awaiting the return of the boats, was an attraction of the Salon.   In 1887 she exhibited an admirable male portrait, in 1888 a portrait of a general of the French army and one of a lady of title, and in 1889, a portrait of an eminent member of the Paris bar.   Meanwhile, her production of picturesque subjects has continued during each of her busy summer vacations on the coast.   "The Fisherman's Daughter" is one of Mlle. Salanson's exhibits in the Salon of 1885.

No. 159

FREDERICK A. BRIDGMAN...............Paris

Born at Tuskegee, Ala., 1847. Studied at Brooklyn Art School, and in 1866 with J. L. Gérôme in Paris. In 1873-74 travelled in Algiers, Egypt, and Nubia. Medals, Paris, 1877, 1878. Chevalier of the Legion of Honor, 1878. Elected Member of National Academy, New York. 1881.

200

"A Street in Algiers"

16 x 12

" Mr. Bridgman, penetrating the atelier-Gérôme as a shy, industrious, black-eyed youth, did not at first make a startling impression. He had no means to assert his powers in the eyes of travelling Americans, and open a dashing studio.   In the provincial aristocracy of France, however, he made a more decided effect.   A piece of romance which happened to him near Pont Aven, in Brittany, had the result of opening some of those charming chateau doors which the minor *noblesse* guard so carefully from most intruders.   While sea-bathing in the Bay of Biscay, he saved from drowning a daughter of the Marquis de Moutier.   Introduced by this act of courage to a family of distinction, his residence in France soon became socially agreeable.   Some of the pleasantest attractions of the French country-house were opened to him ; nor were his black eyes and his powers on the violin misplaced."—EDWARD STRAHAN.

Although his first successes were made by European and historical subjects, Mr. Bridgman has, for the past fifteen years, concentrated the best efforts of his art upon Oriental motifs. He has fallen under the fascination of the sun and is never so happy as when he is giving us upon the canvas its vast blaze of radiance, contrasted with the broad and massive shadows, and enhanced by the intensity and brilliancy of color which nature displays under its influence. Algiers and Egypt have found in him a recorder whose pencil could not be surpassed in fidelity, and, it may be added, he has also described their romances and attractions in the literary field with a pen as facile and faithful as his brush.

No. 160

DAVID JOHNSON......................New York

*Born in New York, 1827. Elected member of the National
Academy, New York, 1862. Medal, Philadelphia, 1876.
One of the founders of the Artists' Fund Society.*

160 "Sandwich Notch, White Mountains"

12 X 14

" 'Through Sandwich Notch the west wind sang
  Good morrow to the cotter;
  And once again Chocorua's horn
  Of shadow pierced the water."
  —JOHN GREENLEAF WHITTIER.

Although he confines himself, as a rule, to the pastoral and simple rural
scenes with which his name has become identified by a long record of artistic
merit and success, Mr. Johnson has executed a number of transcripts of the
grander and more dramatic phases of nature with quite as able a hand. Some
of his most notable earlier pictures have had for subjects the picturesque and
rugged mountain scenery of New York and New England. In the White
Mountains he at one period of his career found the motives for many of those
strikingly pictorial and effective canvases which the Switzerland of America
supplies in such abundance. "Sandwich Notch" is one of these. The Notch
is one of a number that divide the mountains into passes that furnish channels
for the rivers that traverse the district, or open basins for the lakes that
reflect in their depths, as in a black mirror, the environing crags and peaks.

No. 161

CHARLES ÉMILE JACQUE.................Paris

*Born at Paris, 1813. Early in life studied with a geographical
engraver. Later, spent seven years in the army, and worked
two years in England as an engraver on wood. Is famous
for his etchings as well as his paintings. Medals, Paris,
1861, 1863, 1864, 1867. Chevalier of the Legion of Honor,
1867.*

"Sheep and Landscape"

16 x 20

"His inns, his farms, and poultry yards, his village streets, his
skirts of forest, his old walls full of crevices, of stains of damp and
crumbling plaster, his barns with cobwebs hanging from their ceilings, are full of the familiar sentiment of life, as also are of poetry
his far-away twilight skies. Not less does he catch the distinctive
detail of the movement, action, attitude, and relations of animals.
Jacque, who is high in rank among the painters of landscape and
animals, who excels in both, harmonizes the two with true feeling."
—C. H. STRANAHAN, 1888.

Sheep were ever the choice of Jacque as subjects for his brush. He has
painted cattle with equal art, and revelled in the delineation of pigs and barn-
yard fowl. But it is in the sheep that he has found his favorite motives. In
the stall or pasture, penned in the fold or browsing in the freedom of nature,
watched only by the shepherd and his dog, the bleating flocks have found in
him an appreciative historian. His first great successes at the Salon were won
by his sheep pictures. A year ago, when, after fifteen years of absence from
the Salon, necessitated by the rapid transfer of his pictures from his easel to
private galleries, he found time to execute a work for that exhibition, it was
again a flock of sheep with which he called upon the public of the present to
confirm the verdict of the public of the past, a challenge which was promptly
met and responded to in his honor.

No. 162

ERNST MEISSNER...................... Munich

Born in Dresden, 1837. Pupil of Ludwig Richter and Kummer. Entered as a pupil at the Munich École des Beaux Arts, 1870.

230

"The Storm Driven Flock"

29 x 40

" The sounds that drive wild deer and fox
  To shelter in the brake and rocks,
  Are warnings which the shepherd ask
  To dismal and to dangerous task.
  His flock he gathers, and he guides
  To open downs and mountain sides,
  Where, fiercest though the tempest blow,
  Least deeply lies the drift below."

—SIR WALTER SCOTT.

Writing of Meissner, Friedrich Pecht, the great Munich critic, says : " Meissner belongs among the painters of the idyllic life of the fields. From his advent in Munich he attracted attention with his sheep pictures, and he secured an enviable reputation by his ' Winter' in the Dresden Gallery, his ' Stampeded Sheep' in the Vienna Academy, and others. Like Schenck, he gives a dramatic touch to his compositions, and invests them with a sentiment independent of their merely pictorial effect." Here we see the flock buffeted by the blasts of a winter storm, shuddering around the shepherd who guides them to shelter. The feeling of inclement weather, of biting blast and penetrating cold, is made more positive and powerful by the action and expression of man and beast, who in the midst of this frost-bound landscape heighten its sense of desolation by the contrast of their houseless misery.

3

No. 163

ALPHONSE-MARIE DE NEUVILLE (deceased)

Born at St. Omer, 1936. *Pupil of Laurient and Delacroix.
Medals,* 1859, 1861. *Cross of the Legion of Honor,* 1873.
Officer of the Legion of Honor, 1881. *Died,* 1885.

"Wounded Soldier"

(Pen Drawing)

12 X 10

" De Neuville has freedom, audacity, movement, truth of physiognomy, truth of gesture, truth of color at the end of his brush, and all without visible effort. In a word, he has that entirely French quality, the genius of action."—ERNEST DUVERGIER DE HAURANNE.

Struck down in the heat of combat, a soldier has fallen at the feet of his comrades. It is an every-moment incident in the great tragedy of war. The ranks break for an instant. Then they close up again into a living wall as before. Dying or dead, it is all the same, in the sinister system of battles, what has befallen the stricken man. It is enough that he is out of the fight and that another must take his place. A brief touch of a pitying hand, a word of encouragement and cheer from one who may be the next victim of the chances of the fray, and the deadly game goes on, to be played at any cost of blood and honor to the end. M. de Neuville's drawing is a study made by himself for one of those smaller pictures in which he represented the vicissitudes and trials of military life with a strong and sympathetic hand.

No. 164

AUGUST-FRÉDÉRIC-ALBRECHT SCHENCK, Paris

Born at Glückstadt (Holstein), 1828. Pupil of Cogniet. Medal, Paris, 1865. Cross of the Legion of Honor, 1885. Medal, Philadelphia, 1876.

" Sheep in the Snow "

18 x 26

" Albert Schenck is certainly one of the most original figures of the contemporaneous artistic gallery. He is one of those originals of a species not yet extinct, who prefer dogs to men and find more sweetness in sheep than in women. Retired to Écouen, to a farm, he lives in the midst of oxen, dogs, goats, asses, horses, and sheep of all types, races, and species ; cares for them, cultivates them, loves them, and, above all, studies them as never artist studied his models. By means of studying closely the joys and griefs of these modest companions and humble servants of man, he has penetrated the innermost recesses of their souls, which he knows how to show us in pictures of striking truth."—*Le Figaro, June* 5, 1878.

Despite the variety of subjects from animal life to which his pencil has been devoted, it will be by his sheep pictures that Schenck will always be judged at his best and held in the most enduring recollection. That his own predilection is for this submissive and gentle species of the race of brutes, his artistic treatment of it clearly shows. His sheep are invariably made the actors in some more or less dramatic episode familiar to their simple existences and delineated by him with a power of expression and a sympathy of sentiment that could not be greater were they bestowed upon the human race itself. In representing the winter trials and perils of the fleecy flock, the artist touches the level of actual tragedy, and his works in this vein laid the foundation of his fame.

No. 165

EUGÈNE JOSEPH VERBOECKHOEVEN (deceased)

Born in Warneton (West Flanders), July 8, 1799. Medals at Paris, 1824, 1841, and 1855 ; Legion of Honor, 1845. Chevalier of the Order of Leopold, St. Michael of Bavaria, and Christ of Portugal. Decoration of the Iron Cross. Member of the Royal Academies of Brussels, Antwerp, and St. Petersburg. Died, 1881.

" In the Pasture "

7 X 10

" Balthazar Ommeganck has left us landscapes which were much praised in his day. They are picturesque ; his trees are traced with great delicacy, and he evinces a true appreciation of nature. The great care which he bestowed on his shepherds and their flocks earned for him the name of the ' Racine des Moutons,' nor, indeed, is the title inappropriate, for his sheep are painfully elaborated and their fleeces white and lustrous. Nevertheless, this name might be applied with still greater truth to Eugène Verboeckhoeven, the most celebrated among the pupils of Ommeganck."—A. J. WOUTERS.

Extensively as he is famed as a painter of sheep, Verboeckhoeven was, in fact, a master in the widest range of animal painting. His knowledge of the forms, characteristics, and habits of the brute creation was based upon close and constant study from nature, and from the humblest domestic animals to the noblest leaders of the horned herd and the most spirited specimens of the royal equine race, he drew and painted them with equal readiness and accuracy. It is told of him that he enjoyed the painting of horses especially, and that this is true is shown by the fact that some of his best and most striking productions are of this class. His horses are distinguished by character, action, and fidelity of drawing, and he brought to their delineation the same care of execution and elaborateness of detail as mark his other works, and which have obtained for him an unique distinction and popularity among the painters of his time.

No. 166

WILFRED CONSTANT BEAUQUESNE

Born at Rennes.   Pupil of Vernet and Lecomte.

" The Escape "

30 x 34

" The Prussians had, however, reckoned without their host. Having penned us in the old chateau and found it impossible to invade the walls we so effectually defended, they invested the park itself, which was enclosed in a high stone wall.   The situation was critical.   Once they obtained a reinforcement we were certainly doomed by mere force of numbers.   Escape was our only hope. We scaled the park wall near the main gateway, overpowered the drowsy sentry before he could utter a cry, and when the enemy forced the, to their astonishment, undefended gate, it was to find the nest empty and the birds flown."—MONTMORENCY : "*Episodes of the War.*"

The scene described by Captain Montmorency is vividly realized by the artist. He shows the exterior of the wall of the chateau.   Dawn is just breaking. The sombre shades of the forest are rendered darker by the growing luminosity of the sky.   At his post in front of the gateway the Prussian sentry is seen in an attitude of weariness.   Over the wall in the foreground the beleaguered Frenchmen drop, one by one, stealthy, noiseless, like phantoms of the darkness fleeing the approach of day.   In a moment more the sentinel will be overpowered, a dead man will lie among the fallen leaves, and the prisoners of the night will be in full flight, leaving to the enemy, confident of their capture, only an empty old house on which to wreak their chagrin and disappointment in impotent wrath.

No. 167

ÉMILE AUGUST PINCHART..............Paris

Born at Cambrai.   Pupil of Gérôme.   Medal, 1884.

"At the Fountain"

18 x 12

" Pinchart has given us some charming pictures, conceived in an idyllic vein.   In decorative compositions he is most successful.   He has the decorative eye which sees and seizes upon opportunities for pictorial composition independent of those artistic qualities that invite the painter of subject pictures or studies of nature."—" *Gazette des Arts Décoratifs.*"

One of the painter's characteristic decorative compositions, this canvas reveals, in a spring landscape made vivacious by a breezy sky, a female figure at a rustic fountain side.   The treatment is broad, the color delicate and fresh, and the work, in its entirety, an excellent example of his style.

No. 168

JAMES McDOUGALL HART..........New York

Born in Kilmarnock, Scotland, 1828. Brother of William Hart,
N.A. Brought to America. 1831. Studied with Schirmer
in Düsseldorf. Elected member of the National Academy,
New York, 1859.

" Landscape and Cattle "
20 x 16

"Of Scottish art, which has produced some fine things in this
country, James McDougal! Hart is a highly creditable incarnation.
Some of our well-known artists have been his pupils. His industry
is something amazing, while his capacity for hard work is unusual.
He has the hearty manners of the best type of his countrymen ; his
wit is fluent and spontaneous ; his good-nature is the same. He likes
cattle as well as landscape, and for cows and oxen he has the fullest
sympathy.

          *   *   *   *   *   *

In his studies of cattle the same easiness is apparent which is so attractive in his more simple landscapes, and when the two are united
the most delightful harmony is observed in every detail."—*G. W.*
Sheldon, and " Art Journal," 1875.

A typical American landscape, delineated with close adherence to the facts
and sentiment of the scene, is what Mr. Hart never fails to send from his
easel. He sees with clear eyes and paints with an honest hand. It is among
the New England pastures, with their fine umbrageous groves, their placid
streams and ponds, their fertile fields, sedate old farms, and distances of blue
hills so perfect in their rural restfulness and peace, that he is especially at
home. Nature in this mood is ever beautiful and ever attractive to the
artist's eye, while to that of the layman it possesses a familiar and enduring
charm, and it is in this field that Mr. Hart has found the material for the
works that have given him his widest reputation and won him his greatest
favor.

No. 169

J. A. WALKER............................ Paris

Born at Calcutta, of French parents.

"Taking Observations"

12 X 20

"Walker occupies a middle ground between the painters of soldiers and the painters of battles. He is not content merely with the representation of models in uniform, but delights as well in the actual movements of war. A Frenchman in everything but birth, he belongs to France both by the quality of his art and by the choice of subjects by which he challenges our attention and commands our esteem."—ARMAND SILVESTRE.

A commanding officer, upon the outposts, is examining the position of the enemy from a favorable point of observation. He has straightened himself in the saddle, field-glass in hand. His orderlies have reined up their horses at a respectful distance. The ground is covered with snow. The sullen winter sky is heavy with the portent of wild weather. The scene is one of utter dreariness, to which the bloody excitement of battle would afford acceptable variety and relief. As in all of Walker's pictures, the principal figure is a portrait of one of his military friends, of whom his works constitute a gallery of picturesque likenesses, treated in an artistic spirit but none the less faithful in their preservation of the salient traits of personal character.

No. 170

ARSÈNE JULES GARDANNÉ

"The Adjutant"

9 x 7

" A young painter with a future is Gardanné. His soldiers have the truthful quality of Detaille and are handled with spirit. He as yet adheres to simple subjects, single figures, and small groups full of character. They are useful preparations for greater things in the future."—"*Le Figaro*," June, 1886.

A souvenir of the military reviews. The adjutant is dismounted, and stands facing the spectator. The figure is spirited, the character excellent, and the attitude and expression life-like and natural.

No. 171

"Dragon en Vidette"

9 x 7

A character study from the *grandes manœuvres*, a trooper on an outpost. The type is well rendered and the vigilance of duty excellently expressed.

No. 172

DAVID COL............................ Antwerp

Born at Antwerp, 1822. · Pupil of De Keyser and Antwerp Acad-
emy. Medal, Vienna Exposition, 1873. Chevalier of the
Order of Leopold, 1875.

"Hard to Persuade"

11 × 9

"To David Col belongs the palm as the chief painter of familiar
incident in the Belgium of to-day. As a rule, men who paint humor
do so at the expense of their technique. They sacrifice art to the artifice
of their subject. Col, however, gives us his subjects fresh from the
easel of a master, conceived in a light mood, but executed seriously, carefully, with nice attention to detail and an exquisite sympathy with the subtle beauties of nature."—EDWARD FÉTIS.

The master has undertaken to vary the morning promenade and give his dog
a bath by tossing a stick into the ditch, for poor Tray to find and fetch ashore
to him. Tray, however, is either in a stubborn mood or his training has been
defective. He has plunged into the water, but he has not captured the object
destined for his seizure, and his disgusted master, cane in hand, threatens, ex-
postulates, and drives him back as he essays to climb the bank, but all in vain.
The distance affords a charming glimpse of simple Netherlandish landscape,
with the outskirts of a village seen across the footbridge which spans the ditch.
The story is told without exaggeration, and the picture is a capital example of
the artist in composition and characterization, in its delicately fresh and vivid
coloring and in the style and finish of its execution.

No. 173

FRITZ ZUBER BUHLER...................Paris

Born at Locle, Switzerland.   Pupil of Grosclaude and of Picot.

"Rosy Youth"

14 x 10

"Rosy is the West,
    Rosy is the South,
    Roses are her cheeks,
    And a rose her mouth."

—ALFRED TENNYSON.

Childhood has been aptly termed by the poet the time of roses.   It is the one period of life in which flowers bloom untouched by a canker of care.   The little maiden of the artist's fancy has her flower-time in her arms and in her heart.   For her all the universe is a garden which no storm has yet invaded, and life a perfumed round of blossom-garlanded pleasure, broken by no rude worldly touch.   The woods are green, the garden beds in blossom, the south wind blows in warm and balmy zephyrs, yet roses, however beautiful, have thorns, as the little flower-gatherer must some time learn to her cost.   The picture, which is painted with all of the artist's purity and brightness of color, and is beautifully typical of the innocent charm of childhood, is characterized by a tenderness of sentiment and execution that is rarely met with in his strikingly spirited work.

No. 174

CESARE DETTI..............................Paris

Born in Rome, 1849. Pupil of the Academy of St. Luke. Chevalier of the Order of the Crown of Italy.

"Reading Music"

16 x 12

" Music ! Oh, how faint, how weak,

    Language fades before thy spell !

Why should Feeling ever speak,

    When thou canst breathe her soul so well ?

Friendship's balmy words may feign,

    Love's are even more false than they :

Ah ! 'tis only Music's strain

    Can sweetly soothe and not betray."

               —TOM MOORE.

Detti, a Roman who had made Paris his home, was a popular artist in Germany, Italy, England, and America, before the Parisian public found him out to be what he is—a painter of distinction, a water-colorist of great facility and merit, and a wit in his art, as in real life. His " Henry III. Received by the Doge Muccinigo," at the Salon of 1882, was his first real Parisian triumph. When this came to him he was already a prosperous man, so that the French· indorsement of what was practically an international verdict was more of a compliment than a benefaction. He accepted it with the gay and caustic humor native to him. " They are not quite blind, after all," he said. Detti's large historical compositions are few, and painted only for the great exhibitions. In works of moderate and cabinet size he is represented wherever collections of pictures exist, always, as in his " Reading Music," with an abundance of human nature, inspired by his own gayety, and executed with French vivacity and that plenitude of color in which the Italian artist of the present revels as in the sunshine of his native land.

No. 175

JAN VAN CHELMINSKI.................Munich

Born at Brzostov, Poland, 1851. Pupil of Munich Academy and of Franz Adam. Had a studio during 1884-85 in New York.

"The Fugitive Nihilist"

36 x 64

"Mr. Chelminski shows in his canvases a fine instinct for composition and a good eye for character and form. He is a painter of action by inclination, and has a masterly command of movement and physical expression. He draws with grace, ease, and spirit, and his technique is characterized by the same readiness and absence of effort. He possesses the faculty of endowing his figures, human or brute, with a robust and healthy vitality, as well as an admirable distinctiveness of personality. His color is lively and fresh, well regulated, well balanced, and pleasing. At a recent exhibition of his paintings at the Lotos Club, the picture which perhaps attracted most attention was his 'Flight of a Nihilist.' The picture is impressive and full of action."—*"Art Amateur," February,* 1885.

The snow lies deep and crusted on the steppes. The day dies in the sky in flushes of lifeless color without the mellowness or warmth of sunset. The outrider has ignited the tar and tallow-soaked tow in his lantern, and leads the furious flight of the fugitive whose sledge sweeps over the frozen earth in all the frantic haste of a race for life or death. Pursuit is close at hand. Over a ridge, in the undulating waste, the head of a band of Cossacks appears. It is a mere question of speed and the endurance of the panting brutes on whom speed depends. Out of the black shadow of falling night into which the flying patriot is speeding the light of liberty flashes like a beacon. Behind him is the gloom of hopeless servitude or violent dissolution. Such episodes as this are commoner in the history of the Russia of to-day than is the ability of artists to represent them.

No. 176

POMPEO MASSANI

"A Pleasant Passage"

14 X 10

"The Italian sense of humor is active in him, but not to a sufficient extent to invest his works with that element of exaggeration
which mars so much that is otherwise good in modern Italian painting. It expresses itself rather in his rendition of character than in
his subjects themselves. Massani is one of the very few Italians of
our time who can paint a smile. As a rule, his compatriots in art
render it as a guffaw or a grin."—SMITH : *"Report on Art in Italy,"*
1887.

A genial old amateur on the violin has seated himself to the study of a new
score. He has fiddled through the introduction, and for the moment laid his
bow to rest in order to study the notes of a passage in which he evidently finds
an unusual degree of satisfaction. His eyes sparkle. His face wreathes itself
into a smile. Already, in his imagination, he hears himself drawing the notes
he is reading from his instrument, and he smacks his lips at the illusion as a
gourmet might at the anticipation of a feast. Admirable in character and
expression, the picture is also strong and vivacious in color. The complexion
of the amateur has a healthily florid tinge. His sumptuous costume, with its
coat of buff satin and the rich surroundings, show him to be a person well
equipped for the indulgence of any taste his fancy may incline him to. They
also present the artist in the ripeness of his power as a master of color, an expert
in composition, and a student of human nature who reads his lessons with clear
eyes.

No. 177

ARTHUR QUARTLEY (deceased)

Born in Paris, 1839, of English parents. Brought to the United States as a child. Marine painter, self taught. Elected A.N.A., 1878 ; and N.A., 1886. Died, May 19, 1886.

"A Breezy Day in New York Bay"

21 x 16

" And suddenly there springs
Upon the wide sea plain
A breeze like fanning wings,
And life revives again.
And, wavelet on wavelet, the tide
Races on through the harbor wide."

—LEWIS MORRIS.

The charm of brisk movement and variety of color and shifting light and shade that belongs to a breezy day at sea had ever a strong influence on the painter of "A Breezy Day." Some of his happiest and most successful efforts are associated with delineations of this phase of nature, both from the familiar waters of our harbor and the remoter portions of the coast along which he made his studies. New York Bay, from its accessibility, was a favorite source of inspiration with him, and he studied it in all its aspects, friendly and severe, regardless of any inclemency of weather or the discomforts of seasons when artists, as a rule, are content to revive memories of nature in the snug seclusion of their studios. This picture, painted on commission for the owner, and at the painter's strongest period, is as characteristic of its creator's talent as it is of the scene which it depicts.

No. 178

CHARLES FREDERICK ULRICH......New York

Born at New York, 1858. *Studied at National Academy. Later in Munich under Löfftz and Lindenschmidt from* 1873-81. *Elected A.N.A.,* 1883.

"The Lace Worker"

16 x 12

" Yon cottager, who weaves at her own door,
　Pillow and bobbins all her little store ;
　Content, though mean, and cheerful, if not gay,
　Shuffling her threads about the livelong day,
　Just earns a scanty pittance, and at night
　Lies down secure, her heart and pocket light."

—WILLIAM COWPER.

In certain rural communities lace-making forms an employment of those leisure hours which the poor can never afford to pass in idleness, and adds appreciably to the meagre earnings of the household. It is such a worker at this delicate and tedious task that Mr. Ulrich depicts. This picture is one of a series of industrial subjects which the artist executed in the period between his return to America from European study and his departure, later, for Venice, where he has resided for some years. His idea was to present the picturesque side of the daily record of toil, to show the blacksmith at his forge, the carpenter at his bench, the weaver at his loom, the paper-box girl at her work-table, and demonstrate in each and every instance that there is, in the most commonplace and unromantic employment, an interest and a pictorial quality well worth portrayal. He did not carry his purpose as far as he intended, though he did produce a series of pictures on these lines, of which " The Lace Worker " is an admirable example, as it also is of the artist's charm of pure and refined color and his command of the luminous and penetrating effects of light.

No. 179

ÉTIENNE PROSPER BERNE-BELLECOUR.. Paris

Born at Boulogne, June 29, 1838. Pupil of Picot and F.
Barrias. Medals, Salon, 1869, 1872, 1878. Legion of
Honor, 1878. Honorable Mention, 1886.

"Le Capitaine"

16 x 10

" He is a painter of battles at long range.   At the Battle of Malmaison, where the Artists' Brigade was engaged, many were killed or
wounded.   Berne-Bellecour painted a picture of this engagement,
with portraits of some of the regiment—Leroux wounded, Jacquet
firing a last shot, Cuvelier supported by comrades.   In the extreme
distance was the Prussian army, represented by a line of smoke and
a few microscopic figures.   Berne-Bellecour finishes with the utmost
detail the backgrounds of earth fortification and barricade.   These
accessories are not easy to obtain in times of peace, and, in order to
render truthfully his work, he models miniature earthworks of clay,
small timbers and stones, after hasty pen and ink sketches which he
had made during the war.   Berne-Bellecour is tall and well-propor-
tioned, has a fine, military bearing, and might easily be an officer of
the legions he depicts."—HENRY BACON.

The painter renders individual types of military life with the same accuracy
and spirit as he brings to the representation of the greater episodes of that
life itself. His old soldiers are all veritable old campaigners, tanned by the
smoke of battle and toughened by the vicissitudes of long marches and war-
fare in many climes. It is such a character he presents to us in "The Captain," a grim and stanch veteran, to whom death is a playmate, and danger a
trifle to be juggled with as a child might trifle with a toy. In time to come
these admirable bits of individual portraiture will give to Berne-Bellecour
almost as high a place among the character painters of the French army as
his more ambitious and historical compositions have already won for him
among its historians.

4

No. 180

WILFRED BEAUQUESNE

Born at Rennes.   Pupil of Vernet and of Lecomte.

"Attacking the Hospital Train"

32 x 26

" The streets of the village were narrow, and opening upon them were many passage-ways leading into the interior court-yards of the houses. A more favorable place for an ambuscade could not be conceived. Still, we had no occasion to suspect the presence of an enemy so far out of the army's line of march, and though we advanced with caution it was in no special dread of surprise. Suddenly a shot rang out, then another and another. In a moment more we were overwhelmed by a furious assault of the Prussians, made more horrible by the screams of the wounded, who were massacred in the wagons on their beds of straw."—" *Recollections of a Sous-Officier,*" 1869-70.

The painter is said to have been an eye-witness of this incident, which was, by reason of the brutality of such an attack, one of the great sensations of the Franco-Prussian War. Whether he obtained his idea of it from observation, or merely called upon his imagination to assist in its illustration, he has certainly produced a most vivid and spirited picture. The confusion of a surprise, the fury of a desperate contest at close quarters, are admirably rendered by him. The coloring is rich and powerful, the effect striking, and the *mise en scène* has all the picturesqueness of one of those ancient French villages, where generation after generation has housed under the same roof, and only time has wrought any changes in their abodes and surroundings.

No. 181

J. SOULACROIX

/ ʒ ʊ "A Bit of Scandal"

16 x 12

" *Snake :* She wants that delicacy of tint and mellowness of sneer which distinguish your ladyship's scandal.

" *Lady Sneerwell :* You are partial, Snake.

" *Snake :* Not in the least. Everybody allows that Lady Sneerwell can do more with a word or look than many can with the most labored detail, even when they happen to have a little truth on their side to support it.

" *Lady Sneer. :* Yes, my dear Snake ; and I am no hypocrite to deny the satisfaction I reap from the success of my efforts."

—SHERIDAN : " *The School for Scandal.*"

The artist transfers the scene of the famous English comedy to France, but the subject and the period remain about the same. In an interior of the time of the Directoire, hostess and visitor are exchanging the latest tid-bits of social gossip, their budgets being additionally enriched by a contribution in the shape of correspondence which the mistress of the house reads to her friend, with proper interjectory comments thereupon, you may be sure. That this afternoon's conversation will awaken no malicious echoes in Parisian *salons* would be as unreasonable to suppose as that the pleasant little reunions of *Lady Sneerwell* and her friends were without results upon the circle they enlivened, if they did not exactly adorn it.

No. 182

GEORGE H. McCORD, A.N.A..........New York

Born in New York, 1840.   *Pupil of Prof. Morse.*   *Elected A.N.A.*, 1880.

"Near St. Augustine, Fla."

12 X 20

" The beacon light
In red and white
Flashes its flame upon the dusky wave ;
A sentry bright
That through the night
Holds lonely watch, to guide, to warn, to save
The wanderer from a lost and unmarked grave."

—ALFRED AUSTIN.

Mr. McCord is more generally known as a painter of familiar northern land-scape than as a wanderer enriching his sketch-book in remoter fields. The present canvas is a souvenir of a southern tour which resulted in some works of a similarly picturesque character from his easel. He reproduces the local color and the spirit of the scene in them as skilfully as in his translations of nature nearer home. The drowsy charm of a southern twilight, the luxuri-ance of sub-tropical verdure, the richness of color in earth and sky which dis-tinguish a climate where almost perpetual summer reigns, are reflected in them through the sympathy of a temperament which regards nature not only as a mere substantial fact, to be photographically reproduced, but as a source of inspiration, replete with sentiment and rich in the poetry that sensitive souls distinguish in the penetrating influences of the forest and the field.

No. 183

VICTOR BINET..........................Paris

*Born at Rouen.　Pupil of Jacque.　Honorable Mention, 1881.
Medal, 1882, 1883.*

"A Pleasant Pasture"

27 x 33

" The pupils of Jacque are so few that any one of them is worth
chronicling. Of these Binet is probably the most notable. He is,
if anything, a better colorist than his master. He treats landscape
with much feeling and cattle with a touch suggestive of Troyon
rather than his actual preceptor. A worthy artist, it is gratifying to
note that Binet's works find acceptance among our connoisseurs and
that he does not have to go abroad for appreciation."—ÉMILE LE-
CLERCQ.

A characteristic feature of French landscape is the wide and sunny pasturages that environ the settlements of the rural districts. These common
pastures present many subjects for pictures. Even where the orchard growths
take root the turf is by no means allowed to go to waste, for where grass
grows sheep and cattle may be fattened. Economy is part of the French
peasant's nature, and he utilizes every inch of soil to its fullest capacity, for his
horror of waste has become a religion to him. It is one of these communal
pasturages that Binet's picture represents. Here is it that the cattle of the
village graze. Some cows and calves are enjoying the freedom of the green-
sward, wandering at their will. A peasant woman follows the beaten path
across the pasture to the village. Overhead a summer sky, blue as turquoise,
has its heat tempered by cool banks of cloud, and the landscape extends, level
and serene, to the horizon, in itself a picture of rural peace and security in
which the kine may well find pleasant pasturage.

No. 184

PAUL VERNON (deceased)

"At the Brookside"

14 x 18

" Perhaps no pupil ever approached his master in modern times as closely as Vernon approaches Diaz.   Whether through sympathy or imitation, conscious or unconscious as it may be, the former has produced pictures which might readily be called the works of the great hand from which he had his lessons.   Vernon has, apparently, mastered the secret of Diaz's color.   In his wood interiors the resemblance is particularly close.   His figures always remind one of sketches by Diaz."—*London Art Journal*, 1884.

A group of modern wood-nymphs has gathered by a purling brook, as these modern dryads will gather in pictures if not in real life. The slumberous fastnesses of the forest are their best guard against intrusion. No new Actæon will, we may be sure, surprise these modern Dianas at their bath. The artist has limned them from the mirror of his imagination, and their vivid color and vital spirit they owe to him alone. The picture is a very superior example of Vernon, both as a painter and for its approximation to the richness of style and pigment of his master.

/8

No. 185

G. GUZZARDI...........................Florence

"In the Wine-Cellar"

30 X 21

" Fill the goblet again ! for I never before
Felt the glow which now gladdens my heart to its core ;
Let us drink !—who would not ?—since through life's varied round
Iu the goblet alone no deception is found.
I had friends !—who has not ?— but what tongue will avow
That friends, rosy wine ! are so faithful as thou ? "

—Lord Byron.

"Good wine," says Sancho Panza, "is the next best thing to a light heart, and one is as easy to carry as the other." The maxim of Don Quixote's squire finds even more general acceptance in Italy, where they say in a popular proverb, "Water is good for cattle to drink and fish to swim in." Italian art embalms the bibulistic exploits of the nation. The wine-bibber and the wine-drinker are favorite subjects with the artist. Signor Guzzardi presents them to us in their very stronghold—a joyous band of men-at-arms who, in the ripe libations of the time-seasoned casks, are drowning the memories of the hardships and vicissitudes of their campaigns. The vaulted gloom of the wine-cellar reëchoes the boisterous jest and the lusty song. It is a revel indulged in with the whole heart, satisfied with the frolic and the feast of to-day and reckless of any evil, care or trouble that to-morrow may bring forth.

No. 186

WILLIAM M. HARNETT .... New York

Born at Philadelphia, 1851. *Studied at National Academy,*
N. Y. ; also in Frankfort and Munich, 1880–84.

" Still Life "

12 × 15

"The artist shows the highest skill in the representation of textures. The wood is wood, the iron is iron, the brass is brass, the
leather is leather. The technique of these paintings is simply
perfect. The management of light, shade and harmony of color in
these works has reached a point of perfection which amounts to
complete illusion."—*New York World.*

The popularity of the most remarkable painter of still life in America came
to him almost over-night. He had long been producing a series of the most
strikingly deceptive experiments in the delineation of inanimate objects, which
a few connoisseurs, confident of the future of his talent, had acquired as they
were completed, when one of his exhibits at the National Academy of Design
fascinated the always capricious fancy of the public : the newspapers took him
up, and his permanent popularity was assured. A number of larger canvases,
calculated for purposes of illusion and painted for display in public under art-
ful arrangements of light and surroundings, have brought him a decidedly sensational and wide-spread consideration ; but it will be upon his cabinet studies,
so marvellous in their reproductions of form, color and texture, and their
semblance of the solid quality of nature, that his reputation will chiefly rest.

No. 187

J. G. BROWN, N.A.....................New York

*Born in England, 1831. Studied in Newcastle-on-Tyne and
at the Royal Scottish Academy, Edinburgh ; later, with
Thomas Cummings, N.A., in New York. Elected member
of the National Academy, New York, 1863. Medals, Bos-
ton and San Francisco. President of the American Water-
color Society. Honorary member of the Salmagundi
Sketch Club.*

$3/0$

"Nary a Red"

24 X 16

" Although a republic, America possesses one king. This is the
New York street-boy—the Gavroche of the Western Continent, who
is literally monarch of the situation and of all he surveys. He is
inimitable, and Mr. J. G. Brown, the greatest of American figure
painters, paints him as he is, in every phase of his varied industry
and idleness."—GEORGE AUGUSTUS SALA.

That the painter of " Nary a Red " adopted the street-boy as a stock model
out of genuine liking for and sympathy with his individuality and independence
of character he has frequently asserted, and the hearty spirit in which he paints
him bears out this assertion to the letter. To such a young soldier of fortune
as this one, for example, the conquest of the world is but a matter of time. The
universe is for him simply one illimitable possibility, and life a lottery whose
grand prize may be the millions of a magnate of speculation or the power of a
monarch of politics. Fortune is a true coquette. She is never coy to the philosopher who commences life by defying her with a laughing face and a light
heart, and the artist has endowed his little hero with both. The picture, in its
strength and ripeness of color, is an unusually striking example of the best
period of Mr. Brown's art.

No. 188

AUGUSTIN FRANÇOIS ROUMÉGOUS......Paris

Born at Revel, France, 1851. Pupil of Cabanel.

" The Challenge "

40 X 33

" Roumégous comes to us from the South. The hot blood of his nativity has not been chilled by the cool serenity of a course of study under Cabanel. Grounded in his art in Paris, he has been perfected in it in Algiers, whence he brings us the ' Coup de Sirocco,' a canvas worthy of all the notice it receives. Perhaps in order to convince us of his versatility he exhibits at the same time a portrait of a lady, which is equally admirable."—SERRAMINE : "*The Salon of* 1879."

In the inner court-yard of an Oriental habitation a furious brawl has broken out between the master of the house and an intruder. The latter stands with his back to the spectator, in a posture of sturdy defiance. The sunlight flashes on the bare blade of his scimetar. The master is restrained in his doorway by his servants and dependents, with whom he struggles fiercely to escape and accept the challenge hurled at him by his enemy. The lofty walls of the house lose themselves above. A flood of the radiance of noonday pours down into the court, mapping out its picturesqueness in masses of strongly contrasted light and shadow. The action of the scene is as vivid as its setting. This picture was painted by the artist, who is now a resident of New York, since his arrival in America, and is a reminiscence of an incident of his last tour of North Africa.

No. 189

WILLIAM HART, N.A.................New York

*Born in Scotland, 1822. Elected Member of National Acad-
emy, New York, 1858.*

"Landscape and Cattle"

18 x 14

" William Hart's style is rich and glowing, and for subjects he
prefers the brilliancy of a sunset sky, or the delineation of the gorgeous tints of autumn foliage, or Nature in her brightest rather than
in her dark and gloomy phases.   As Tuckerman remarks in his
' Book of the Artists,' his landscapes ' admirably discriminate the
diversities and coincidences of natural phenomena in North Britain
and North America ; they display characteristic features, often rendered with consummate taste.   His pencil is alike chaste and living.
true and tender, and many of his smaller landscapes are gems of
quiet, yet salient beauty.' "—*Art Journal*, August, 1875.

A corner of a New England pasture, shaded by verdure in its richest dress
bathed in the light of a faultless day of Indian summer, and made sumptuous
in color by the fruition of the ripest season of the year, is what Mr. Hart presents to us in this canvas.   All of the elements of nature that have invited him
to his most noteworthy work are present in this subject.   The composition is
one of great natural charm ; the scenery has a friendly and familiar character.
and the execution is worthy of the artist in the ripeness of his powers.   The
cattle are painted, as is usual with the artist, with a breadth and vigor of
touch that render them, while enlivening the landscape, a picture in themselves, and one which even in these miniature dimensions has the force of a
large canvas.

No. 190

HENRY P. SMITH.....................New York

Born at Waterford, Conn., 1854.   Self-taught.   Landscape and Marine Painter.

"A Winter Gale on the Jersey Coast"

27 x 36

The rough north winds have left their icy caves
>> To growl and group for prey
>> Upon the murky sea ;
The lonely sea-gull skims the sullen waves
>> All the gray winter day.

>> —ELIZABETH STODDARD.

The rough north winds have not only left their icy caves in Mr. Smith's picture, but have found gallant prey as well. The good ship, battling with the merciless and irresistible powers of the tempest, has sailed her last voyage and found a resting place for her doomed hulk upon the lee-shore that seamen dread with such ample reason. Whelmed by the waters of the murky sea, shaken and racked by the fury of the bellowing blast, every surge that sweeps her fated deck assists in the work of inevitable destruction. The roar of the surf, whose titanic assaults shake the frozen shore as if they would batter it to pieces like some frail thing of human workmanship itself, drowns all the sounds of human distress or terror. Death and destruction ride abroad upon the gale, and earth and ocean are theirs until their work is done. To-morrow the sun may shine again, but its beams will warm to life none of the actors in this tragedy of the billows and the blast.

No. 191

AUGUSTE HAGBORG ....Paris

Born at Gothenburg, Sweden.   Pupil of the Academy of Fine Arts, Stockholm, and of Palmaroli, Paris.   Medal, Paris, 1879.

"A Passing Flirtation"

30 x 40

"Of majestic stature, with a handsome and characteristic head, one recognizes in him at once the strong man and the artist, the indefatigable fighter and worker, whose eyes, flashing with inspiration and spirit, have in them still that tenderness which belongs to the Swedish eye, tinted with the beautiful blue of the sea.   Everything is robust and vigorous in the talent which confirms him as one of the masters of the future."—*Auguste Hagborg,* by A. M. DE BÉLINA.

It is a mere interchange of empty badinage and the rude wit of the shore that passes between these sturdy fisher-lasses and the lusty lad whose path on the wide wet sands has crossed their own—a flirtation as capricious and as free as the breeze that stirs the sea and sweeps the sky.   There is no malice in such coquetry as this to leave a sting.   Men and nature are alike in that gray North that Hagborg paints so well ; frank, bold, self-reliant, honest to themselves and all the world, they preserve in their simple, healthful and straightforward lives much of the unconscious dignity of that older civilization which modern refinement has polished out of existence in less primitive and more advanced and artificialized communities.

No. 192

JEAN GEORGE MEYER VON BREMEN (deceased)

*Called, from his birthplace, Meyer von Bremen. Born October
28, 1813. Pupil of Sohn. Member of the Amsterdam
Academy. Gold Medal of Prussia, 1850. Medals at Berlin
and Philadelphia.*

"The Artist's Studio"

32 x 16

"When young Jean George Meyer emerged from the Düsseldorf
Academy in 1842 to install himself in the dignity of a studio of his
own, it was as a painter of religious works of the largest size that he
aspired to fame. It was not long before he discovered that his talent
had mistaken its direction. His heart was not in these academic and
artificial compositions, while all around him nature—and above all,
human nature—invited him to more congenial fields. So the painter
of tradition soon became the painter of fact, and his exquisite little
cabinet pictures of domestic scenes and homely episodes of every-day
life were not long in securing favor. One of the earliest and most
successful of his efforts in this new direction was an interior scene
in his own studio, which possesses the additional charm and value of
presenting portraits of himself and family in the naïve and attractive
grouping of a picture."—HEINRICH CARL VON LIEDENAU.

It is of this picture that the distinguished German critic and essayist writes
so appreciatively. In his studio, irradiated by a pleasant glow of sunlight, the
artist is seated at his easel. His wife, in the freedom of complete and perfect
sympathy and confidence, criticises and suggests upon the work on which he is
employed, while his children complete at once the composition and the family
group. The portraiture is said to be excellent. The picture, mellow in color
and rich in the variety of its accessories, has all the attractiveness of an imag-
inative work, as well as the more intimate and personal interest associated
with a glimpse of the home life of one of the great artists of the century.

No. 193

ÉTIENNE PROSPER BERNE-BELLECOUR, Paris

Born at Boulogne June 29, 1838. Pupil of Picot and F. Barrias. Medals, Salon, 1869, 1872, 1878. Legion of Honor, 1878. Honorable Mention, 1886.

"The Embarkation"

21 x 32

" Berne-Bellecour is not one of those painters of battles whose field of experience is the studio. Up to 1870 he was a painter of anything—everything—but war. But when the war of 1870 broke out, he promptly returned from Algiers, where he was painting, and enlisted in the Francs-Tireurs of the Seine. He had for comrades Jacquet, Leloir, Vibert, Jacquemart, and Le Roux. The rigors of the service were relieved by the pleasures of the pencil. When he had not to shoulder his musket his sketch-book was in his hand. Between sketches and skirmishes life took flight with him like the smoke of the battle-field before the breeze, until the fight at Malmaison. Here the artists distinguished themselves. The sculptor Cuvelier was killed ; Le Roux had a leg smashed by a cannon ball ; Berne-Bellecour, untouched, received for his gallantry the military medal of honor."—SAVARY : *"Art Under Arms."*

Times have changed since a movement of troops to the front meant long forced marches, in which were wasted precious hours and days upon which the fate of a nation often hung. The railroad has simplified matters nowadays, and reduced the calculation of time from the embarkation to the arrival to an exact computation of minutes and seconds. They can, no doubt, tell you at the War Office just when M. Berne-Bellecour's regiment is due at the line of battle, and at what hour of the clock its chassepots should be giving an account of themselves at the enemy's expense. It is to be noted that this picture, for character of composition and the number of figures in it, is one of the most important that has left the artist's easel.

No. 194

JEAN JACQUES HENNER..................Paris

Born at Bernwiller (Alsace) 1829. Pupil of Drölling and Picot.
Won the grand Prix de Rome, 1858. Medals, Paris, 1863,
1865, 1866, 1878; Cross of the Legion of Honor 1873; Officer
of the same, 1878.

" Ideal Head "

10 x 8

" This powerful master has ever loved to paint youth, beauty, woman in all of her that is seductive and charming, maidens whose adolescent forms are full of grace, nymphs with skins of milk, and goddesses with flesh of ivory. He has been compared to Giorgione, to Correggio, to Rembrandt, to Philippe de Champagne ; but he remains always himself, serene and unapproachable. In his brilliant artistic career Henner has never sacrificed his individuality for a moment, and never relaxed his quest for the ideal, whose search he has marked with a succession of masterpieces."—A. M. DE BÉLINA.

Seen in profile, framed in simple drapery against a background equally simple and equally rich in color, the artist presents to us one of his ideal female types in all the brilliancy of that dazzling purity of complexion which is the keystone of his fame, and which Roger Ballu compared to a white camellia, opening in the sun. Next to the charm of color itself one must admire the firm and yet delicate modelling of the face, conveying as it does the suggestion of the substance and roundness of flesh, without an obvious effort, and the broad and vigorously efficient rendition of the textures in drapery and background. Henner's characteristic technique, like his color, possesses an individual charm.

No. 195

EMIL RAU..............................Munich

*Born in Dresden, 1858. Pupil of Pohle. Went to Munich in
1879, and became a pupil of Alexander Wagner and Lindenschmidt. Since 1883 he has pursued an independent career.
Diploma of honor in Berlin, 1886.*

"A Village Beauty"

26 x 20

" Among painters of peasant life and character Emil Rau attracted
attention in Berlin by his ' Light Cavalry.' The subject represented
a bold and insolent cavalier who, returning from the dance with his
sweetheart and her friend upon his arms, aroused the jealousy of the
former by his flirtation with the latter. The figures were in the size
of life, somewhat flashy and cold in color, but conceived in such a
healthy and humorous spirit and executed in such excellent character,
that the composition did its creator credit and fairly won for him his
diploma of honor."—FRIEDRICH PECHT: *"History of Munich Art."*

She is one of those coquettish beauties over whom the jovial but fiery moun-
taineers of the Bavarian and Austrian Tyrol so often come to blows that are
not seldom reinforced by resort to the bludgeon and the sheath-knife. They
form a race by themselves, these sirens of the highlands, and one that is well
known to the artists of Munich, whose seasons of summer study bring them
into familiar contact with them, and whose canvases, in every exhibition,
record their healthy and substantial charms. The original of Rau's vivid and
life-like subject is, according to the artist's attestation, the daughter of an inn-
keeper in the Salzkammergut, whose captivations of person and capriciousness
of temper have created more trouble in the district of her nativity than would
be caused by a political revolution.

5

No. 196

R. PELLEFIGUE..........................Paris

"At the Review"

18 x 14

" Here is a newcomer in the painted field of war. Shall we see more of him? He begins well, at least, and experience will do the rest. He has ideas and the courage to utter them."—JEAN AUBLET: *" Les Peintres Militaires."*

A scene at a military review. The group of officers, posted on a height of observation, includes military representatives of various nations. The uniforms are to be discovered of German, English, Austrian, Italian, Spanish and Russian officers, as well as of the French, who act as hosts. They are contemplating the movement of the sham fight in an agreeable amity which the next turn of the political wheel may convert into the bitterest and bloodiest international hatred.

No. 197

ALBERT CHARPIN..........................Paris

Born at Grasse in the Alps. Pupil of Daubigny.

//ʃ   **"Under the Willows"**

22 x 30

" Although a pupil of Daubigny, Charpin's pictures suggest more strongly the influence of Corot. There are times when, in his land-scapes, one can almost detect the hand of the master. He adopts the same method of treating light, in a subdued brilliancy and clear-ness of tone, and handles his landscapes in harmony with this method. He studies nature and represents her well."—ARMAND SILVESTRE.

In a group of dwarf willows a flock of sheep is gathered, filling the fore-ground. At the edge of the grove are the shepherd and his dog. The middle ground shows a low lying meadow-land, moist with the overflow of ditches and the settlement of rains. The distance is traversed by a stream. Spring-time freshness of color and coolness of atmosphere invest the composition. The sky is bright without glare. The landscape is treated broadly, but with close observance of its character, the details are competently suggested and the local color so well preserved that one might place the locality of the scene by it alone. The subject is drawn from the upper regions watered by the river Oise, Daubigny's own field of life-long labor and Charpin's chief ground for sketching and study.

No. 198

WILLIAM M. BROWN..................New York

Born in Troy, N. Y., 1827. Painted portraits for a time, but in 1850 turned his attention to landscape. In 1865 began painting fruit, in which he has made a distinguished reputation.

"Winter on the Mohawk"

12 X 18

" Wm. M. Brown is one of a not inconsiderable number of American artists whose reputation ·is largely local.   He was a good portrait painter when, at the age of 23, he turned his attention to landscape.   He was a good landscape painter when he commenced, in 1865, to paint fruit, in which class of still life it was reserved for him to win his most distinguished consideration.   Little known to the public away from his native city of Troy and the adjacent district of this State, his works have been absorbed into private collections as quickly as they were completed, and have found a wide distribution."—*American Art Journal.*

Mr. Brown is here represented by a characteristic work of his second period. It is a midwinter landscape, after one of the heavy snowfalls once commoner to the interior section of New York State than they have been of late years. The historic Mohawk was a favorite and fertile sketching ground with this artist, and he painted it at every season and under every variation of effect : in the fresh bloom of spring, the opulence of midsummer, the fruitfulness of autumn, and in all the dreary picturesqueness of its winter sleep, always with a patient devotion to facts and a painstaking realization of the scene as it presented itself for realization by his brush.

No. 199

HENRY P. SMITH...................New York

Born in Waterford, Conn., 1854. Came to New York at the age of 13. Is self-taught in art.

//0

" Landscape : Connecticut Valley "

14 X 12

" There is a beautiful spirit breathing now
  Its mellow richness on the clustered trees,
  And from a beaker full of richest dyes
  Pouring new glory on the autumn woods."
               —H. W. LONGFELLOW : *" Autumn."*

The season of fruitage has arrived. In the wheatfield the reapers are at work, and the sheaves are being bound and stacked. A mellow glory of color enriches all the scene. The woods show a touch of russet. The distance lies fertile in the sun. The river reflects in its unruffled mirror a sky as soft and tender as a dream, and the long afternoon lingers as if loath to blot out the beauty of the picture. There is no more delightful treasury of purely rural scenery in America than certain sections of New England. The artists discovered this fact long ago, though not all of them realize it as attractively and as faithfully to itself as does Mr. Smith in this thoroughly characteristic canvas. The artist was born among such scenes as this, and their spirit enters into his brush when he depicts them.

No. 200

LEOPOLD SCHMUTZLER...............Munich

*Born in Bavaria. Pupil of Munich Academy. Medals at
Munich, 1883, 1885. Member of the Royal Academy,
Munich.*

"Practising"

15 x 11½

" Her fingers shame the ivory keys,
They dance so light along ;
The bloom upon her parted lips
Is sweeter than the song."

—JOHN GREENLEAF WHITTIER.

It is awfully dull work practising. Who that has essayed the mastery of the
piano's keys has not found this out? From the days when the spinet was what
is to-day the parlor-grand, the story has ever been the same—the hours of
study are never hours of ease. Consequently M. Schmutzler's pretty student
of the harmonies can well be pardoned for lifting her eyes from her instrument
at the sound of an intruding step. Of course it is *his* step—whose else could
it be, to stir the sparkle in those bright eyes or part those lips into such a
smile ? The piano will be troubled no more to-day, that is evident. To-morrow ? Well, perhaps, if *he* does not call too early, with his special version of
the same old story that is ever new.

No. 201

GEORGES HAQUETTE...................Paris

Born at Paris. Pupil of Adolph Millet and of Cabanel. Medal,
1880.

/30

"The Fisherman's Pride"

30 X 22

"Haquette, a child of the town, became by accident only a
painter of the children of the coast. A chance visit to the seaside
laid the foundation of his choice of subjects. The discovery of a
picturesque old fishing boat did the rest. His models he sought at
the seaside. His boat he transported to Paris, where he painted it in
every aspect, position and condition of effect. A legitimate success
attends M. Haquette in his representations of maritime life. To
Pollet, that picturesque quarter which makes Dieppe two distinct
cities, the painter retires during ten months of the year, to study
on the spot the physiognomies he depicts."—*L'Art Contemporaine.*

The hard life of the humble toiler who subsists by the harvest of the sea is
in nothing harder than in the bearing his perilous avocation has upon his domestic existence. It has well been said that the French fisherman takes his
life in his hand whenever he pushes off from the shore, and that he puts himself in the balance of chance against every fish that he entangles in his net.
Times of much labor and of little ease are lived by him and his dependants.
His own career has the excitement of battle to support it. The wife and child,
left behind in doubt and constant dread of the worst which experience has
taught them to expect, find their only moments of rest and peace when the
husband and father is with them, and when his presence renders certain the
fact that the merciless and greedy ocean has not yet claimed him as its prey.

No. 202

J. H. WITT...................   ....New York

*Born in Indiana, 1840.   Studied in Cincinnati.   First exhibited
at National Academy, 1868.   Elected A.N.A., 1885.*

"Sleeping Pets"

27 X 30

"It is in his pictures of children that Mr. Witt is exceptionally
happy.   He seems to enter into their lives with a fine appreciation
of their sentiments and a sympathy with them that are reflected upon
the canvas to which he transfers his impressions.   He is a draughts-
man of sterling merit, a good colorist, refined without weakness,
and as a technician exhibits directness and force.   His fidelity to
facts is that of a student who finds in nature his best model, and it
places him among the foremost detail painters of the day."—"*Representative American Artists.*"

Puss and her little mistress, tired out together, are napping in a cozy corner.
From their close contiguity to each other it is easy to see that they are as good
friends asleep as awake.   Secure in the confidence of well-protected childhood,
the baby sleeps without a dream, while the four-footed pet exhibits a placid
surrender of all the natural watchfulness and care of her race, which augur
favorably for the indulgence allowed her.   The picture is an admirable speci-
men of the artist in the sweetness of its conception, the sentiment with which
it is realized, and the excellence of the technical treatment of the canvas, in
which the painter's best and most popular qualities are reflected.

No. 203

WILFRED C. BEAUQUESNE

Born at Rennes.   Pupil of Vernet and of Lecomte.

"The Honors of War"

22 X 33

" In Beauquesne we have the Doré of our battle-fields.   He sees with a quick eye and records his observations with a rapid hand. War is to him not a matter of detail, but a terrible and tragic whole, and he builds his pictures on this basis.   He has the genius of his master, Horace Vernet, and the spirit of our own time, and among the painters of battles he will hold a perpetual place."— ÉMILE LANSYER.

It is the end of a battle—the end of a victory. Success has crowned the eagles of France, but at what cost !   The remnants of a victorious sortie return to the fortifications, triumphant in the fight, but with bowed heads, for their leader has fallen in the fight.   His corse is borne upon the stretcher shouldered by stalwart guardsmen.   His charger, that shall never feel the pressure of his spur again, is led by his orderly in the van of the cortege.   The procession has the measured solemnity of a death parade.   The soldiers march with drooping heads.   The delvers in the trenches doff their caps.   There are no cheers here to salute the triumph of the hour.   Over the brilliancy of victory death casts a grim shadow, although the sun is shining and the day is fair. The painter has given life to an episode of war that commonly exists only in the cold and methodical descriptions of the reports from headquarters.   He has made living to the eye one of those inevitable incidents of battle which are generally left to the imagination alone.

No. 204

WILHELM KRAY................. ....Vienna

*Born at Berlin.   Spent some time in Rome and Venice, then
settled in Vienna.   Professor in the Royal Academy at
Vienna.*

" The Water-Nymphs' Prey "

30 X 42

" The boat rocked soft on the idle tide,
   The moon's kiss whitened the waters wide,
   The fisher-boy slept in the silver glow,
   While fate wove his web in the depths below :
   Wove his fate of the golden hair
   Of naiad and water-sprite, false and fair."

—WALTHER V. ALBERSBERG.

Kray has constituted himself the chief and most graphic of artistic perpetu-
ators of the quaint old German legends of the water-fairies.   From gentle
Undine and the deadly *Lorelei* down to the sprites that even tradition pro-
vides no name for, he has given the naiads a tangible and fascinating form on
canvas, and a fixed and definite place in art.   Here we see the indolent fisher-
lad of the old song taken by surprise at his neglected task by the water-nymphs,
who deepen his slumber with the spell of their unearthly melody and seduce
him, still dreaming, into the fatal depths from which he shall never return.
Always graceful in composition and striking in effect, with female types of
the greatest purity and elegance of form, Kray's pictures have gained wide
acceptance for their decorative value as well as for the intrinsic interest of
their stories and the artistic excellence of their execution.

No. 205

JOSÉ FRAPPA............................Paris

Born at St. Etienne, France, in 1854. Learned the trade of a designer for silks. In 1874 went to Paris on his savings, and became a pupil of Pils. He later received instruction from Charles Compte and Vibert.

"Over the Garden Wall"

28 x 18

" It was in 1879 that his Salon picture, ' Les Queteurs,' gave José Frappa the place in the estimation of the Parisian public which he still enjoys. The scene was the court-yard of a country house. Perched on the shoulder of one mendicant friar, against the house-wall, another begging brother reached up to kiss, at the window, the hand of a pretty girl who was about to reach him a contribution for his haversack. The tribute might pass with the devout as one of gratitude to charity. The cynical smiled to see in it a tribute of the Church to the boudoir, and Frappa's fortune was made."—PAUL MAHTZ.

It is possibly on account of his early good fortune with the Church for a motive that Frappa still adheres to it in his subjects. Since his first Salon exhibit, in 1876, the monk has been a part of almost all his pictures. Here the figure his clerical hero cuts is that of a marplot. Two lovers in a quiet garden, whose bowers invite confidence and mutual rhapsodies, have been exchanging their vows. In the full heat and fervor of their reciprocal passion the thread of sentiment is rudely snapped. Over the wall above them appears the scep-tical face of a jovial friar who has been tending the fruit trees in the adjoining orchard garden of his convent. The startled pair spring to their feet. In a moment more their eavesdropper will leave them to themselves, no doubt, with an ironical apology for his intrusion. Meanwhile, however, the element of disturbance has done its work and Cupid, for the nonce at least, has taken flight beyond the reach of pious Paul-Pryism.

No. 206

FREDERICK SCHUCHARD, Jr.........New York

Born in New York, 1856.   Studied under William Morgan and
J. G. Brown, 1875–78.   First exhibited at National Acad-
emy of Design, 1877.

"A Cold Day"

32 X 20

"Schuchard is a pupil of Brown who shows the influence of his master rather in the selection of his subjects than in their presentation.   His color is less vivid and vital, but his pictures are excellent in spirit and frequently inspired with a pleasant and thoroughly human humor that lends them a distinctive character."—*American Art Journal*, 1886.

There has been a heavy snow-fall during the night.   The city streets are deep in a white covering of banked and drifted crystals, and the leaden sky suggests a present addition to their burden.   The little street musician is an early riser. He has come abroad with the cheerless dawn and fiddled his salute under windows behind which comfort still blinks at the world with drowsy eyes. His face is good humored and gay with the careless light-heartedness of boyhood.   Like the sparrows harvesting in the snow he trusts to fortune for the sustenance of the day, and does not find his confidence misplaced.   His philosophy is sounder than his shoes, and in his contentment he is richer in his rags than Midas, turning every useful thing he touches into useless gold.

No. 207

CAMILLE MAGNUS

2 t^0

"Greek Girls in the Forest"

14 x 18

" That an art critic should be an artist at heart is but just. That
he should be an artist in fact is less common. In Gautier we have
an example of the painter turned critic. In Camille Magnus we
know the critic becomes a painter. The inclination was born in him.
His educational course caused him to gravitate naturally to literature.
His choice in literature was the chronicling and the criticism of art.
Contact with the artists did the rest, and we behold this writer of
conceded power developed into a painter of no mean ability, whose
pictures are prized for the double merit of intrinsic value and of curiosity as exploits of a man who was constant to his theories that one
should be able to practise the art which one assumes the privilege
to criticise."—Auguste Vitre.

Although the art of Magnus is largely eclectic, being based upon a sympathetic study of the works of many men, the influence of Díaz, who was his
close friend and principal artistic adviser, is most perceptible in his pictures.
That he was a mere imitator of Díaz it would be unfair to state. He painted
in the same vein because his sympathies were of the same order. Both in his
landscapes and his combinations of the figure and landscape he evidences a
command of color that falls little short of that of his master. His " Greek
Girls " is a charming group that shows him at his best as a colorist of power
and a technician of the first order, free and firm of touch and frank in his
expression of facts, transposed rather than translated, according to his own
poetic mood.

No. 208

FRANÇOIS MIRALLES

Born at Valencia, Spain.   Studied at L'École des Beaux Arts, Paris.   Member of the Academy of St. Luke, Rome.

"The Bull-Fighter off Duty"

10 x 8

"He sat a little apart, watching the progress of the sport. He was perfectly at his ease, though evidently fully conscious that the attention of half the enormous audience was divided between him and the fight. He had the aspect of a popular actor, to whom popular adulation was a matter of course. For perfect self-possession, complete self-satisfaction and the serenity of conscious eminence, I had never seen his presence equalled in the experiences of a lifetime spent in wanderings of the world."—MONKHURST : "*Spanish Types and Manners.*"

Modern art has made of the bull-fighter almost as pronounced a character as have the customs of that Spanish life in which he is so important a figure. He is the idol of the nation, worshipped alike by the mob and by the élite ; by the classes with whom the sports of the bull-ring are the only diversion, and by those to whom the doors of the playhouse and the salons of society are open. He wins laurels and amasses fortunes. His amatory conquests rival those of a great tenor, and his appearances in public are accompanied by an amount of attention that would not be misbestowed upon a successful soldier, a conqueror of nations. In his spirited character study Miralles has painted him to the life, gorgeous in his vestments of office and magnificent in his superb acceptance of the honors due to his skill, his intrepidity and his preëminence as the chief factor in the amusement whose cruel picturesqueness has become as much a part of his nation's existence as its religion and its laws.

No. 209

LUDOVIC MOUCHOT...... ....Paris

Born at Poligny, France.   Pupil of Cabanel.

"The New Anthem"

27 X 30

" Mouchot is another of the painters of monks, but he does not satirize them.   He takes them seriously, and they owe him a debt of gratitude for the excellent representations he makes of them at their duties."—MARTIN BLAISEGOFFE.

The convent choir is assembled to rehearse a new composition, composed for some special and important occasion.   The music-master of the monastery acts as leader.   Three of the brethren, seated before their scores, represent the tuneful contingent of the place, and sing under his direction and dictation. The scene is one of the sparsely furnished rooms characteristic of conventual edifices.   The stone wall is panelled at the base, but bare above.   A hanging of tapestry separates the apartment into two spaces.   There are some books of music scattered about, and for the rest the composition depends upon its human adjuncts for interest.   The expression of the singing monks and the seriousness and intentness of their leader are notably expressive features of the picture.   The scene is an interior in one of the historical convents of Paris, and it is a faithful reproduction of the spot.

No. 210

J. P. MORELLI

"The Tambourine Girl"

38 x 29

" I love my little native isle,
    Mine emerald in a golden deep ;
My garden where the roses smile,
    My vineyard where the tendrils creep.
How sweetly glide the summer hours
    When twilight shows her silver sheen,
And youths and maids from all the bowers
    Come forth to play the tambourine."
        —MACKAY : " *The Tambourine Girl of Procida.*"

The painter shows us his tambourine girl among her native bowers at rest; a rustic beauty, strong in health, and with the pensive loveliness that invests the Latin races with an unique charm. The tambourine, whose origin is lost in the mists of antiquity, is to this day the popular instrument of the Biscayan and Italian peasants. It figures in their festivities as importantly as the banjo with the American negro, or the castanets and the guitar in Spain. The skill with which it is performed upon by those to whom its use is, so to speak, second nature, is beyond all powers of verbal description. It is capable of many inflections of sound that can be made harmonious, if not melodious, and its thrilling effect upon the nerves, when adroitly performed in chorus, is doubtless its title to the popular favor it enjoys. It is a sharp spur to the dance with which the Italian peasant is ever ready to conclude the most laborious and exhausting labors of the day.

No. 211

CHARLES T. PHELAN .... New York

Born in New York, 1840. Landscape painter. Pupil of Rondel.

105

"Midsummer"
16 x 22

" Midsummer days, when pastures rich and green,
Decked in the robes of Nature's richest sheen,
Smile to the sky, and when the drowsy bird,
Deep in the covert, is not seen nor heard ;
Days when the sun rules with a power supreme
The panting life of every rustic scene."

—ROBERT BLOOMFIELD.

The uncompromising glare and the uniform color of midsummer have not made it a favorite subject with American landscape painters, who by preference seek their subjects in the spring and autumn seasons. Mr. Phelan has, however, assailed his task fearlessly and carried it to a successful result. Under a blazing sky the landscape swoons in an ecstasy of heat. Even the stream in the foreground reflects the glare of the firmament with no promise of refreshing coolness in its waters. A few sheep and lambs linger listlessly on its marge, too drowsy in the scorching noonday to either browse or drink. Into the burning distance stretches a rolling upland, dotted with farms, and a few trees on the farther bank of the stream provide a shadow that is refreshed by no breath of breeze. The artist has evidently felt the influence of midsummer in this picture as well as studied its superficial indications.

6

No. 212

FEDERICO DIAQUE .... Paris

Born at Madrid.　Studied with his father, Ricardo C. Diaque.

" An Interrupted Interlude "

28 x 36

"Among these painters of studio interiors Diaque is one of the most interesting.　He gives us the usual studies of still life, it is true, but adds to them always a certain human interest.　His color is always good, and he never fails to seize upon what sentiment the subject may hold within itself."—HENRI BELLENGER.

It is the idle hour in the coziest corner of the studio.　The palette has been laid aside and the fair sitter, whose charms the hand of art has been transferring to the canvas, is given an interlude of idleness.　She has fluttered over the last file of the *Petit Journal pour Rire*, and having smiled at its satires and exhausted its *double-entendre* and its witticisms, has tossed it aside to seek in *Le Figaro* some matter of current interest in the gossip of the town.　Time slips by unnoted under such circumstances, and in the midst of the most interesting passage the click of the opening door warns her that her recess is over and the hour of the pose again at hand.　M. Diaque tells his story without effort or exaggeration, and the varied accessories of his scene he paints with equal ease and skill.　His still life plays an important part in the picture, but is completely subordinated to the graceful figure whose unconstrained beauty it furnishes a background for.

No. 213

MAURICE BLUM.......,.......,.............,..Paris

Born at Lyons.   Pupil of Picot and of Eugene Delacroix.

"The Master"

10 x 6

" A painter of decorative pieces. Not without spirit and an appreciation of character. He gives to his little panels a sparkle of color
and excellent drawing and technique. At the Salon he occasionally
shows more ambitious work, well executed."—PELADIN : " *The
Lesser Salon.*"

The music-master is imparting a lesson on the mandolin to an unseen circle
of pupils. All that the artist shows us is the master himself, standing and
twangling the strings of his instrument. He is an elderly gentleman of a mild
aspect and a rapt expression that shows his whole heart to be in his work.
His respectable dress is an augury of a profitable *clientele*. While the sober
black of his breeches, stockings and hat relieve him from any charge of unpro-
fessional foppery, his fawn-colored coat lends him a certain spruce air suggestive that the fair sex is not without representation among those scholars which
we can see with our mind's eye outside the limits of the frame in which his
portrait is enclosed.

No. 214

PIERRE-MARIE BEYLE....................Paris

Born at Lyons, 1838.   Was a house-painter, but was assisted by
the designer, Philippon, and his first picture was admitted to
the Salon in 1867.   Medals, 1881, 1887.

" Booby Rock "

15 X 22

"O wild gray rocks ! O weed-green rocks ! O white rocks wet with
    spray !
By happy waters washed all night, by sunbeams kissed all day,—
Among your rifts a little wave has strayed and lost its way."

—M. C. GILLINGTON.

When Pierre-Marie Beyle ran away from his home at Lyons to join a roving
band of mountebanks whose free and easy life had captivated his boyish fancy,
nothing was, probably, farther from his mind than that he should ever become
a painter.   But the artist was in him and he made his debut as a caricaturist in
Paris, whither he had wandered, under the guidance of the inimitable Philippon, in due time.   In the intervals of his satirical and humorous work, which
enjoyed a marked degree of success with the public, he cultivated the higher
art of painting.   His pictures of fishermen and women, of the life and homely
romance of the coast, commenced to attract an attention which every annual
exhibition added force to, and his reputation was confirmed by a large and important work, representing the return to his home of the body of a drowned
fisherman, borne by his sorrowing comrades.   But he did not confine himself
to tragic and melancholy subjects, and his lighter and more cheerful studies of
coast scenery and characters are full of nature and justly and highly esteemed.

No. 215

FRANCOIS LEONARD JEAN MOORMANS (dec'd)

Born at Rotterdam, 1831. Died 1873. Pupil of the Academy at Antwerp. Medals in various European Exhibitions. Professor in Academy at Amsterdam.

"Luncheon Time"

14 x 10

"A Dutchman of Belgian schooling, in whom, however, the traditions of his race had not entirely expired ; such was Moormans. He painted interiors in a style that would have done credit to a pupil of Van der Meer or of Pieter de Hoogbe, and there are times when his figures have the quality of these masters. He has a unique place in the art of the Netherlands in the Nineteenth Century." --ERNEST CHESNEAU.

In a Dutch interior of the Sixteenth Century an old lady, clad in black and seated at a table, is being served with a simple refection by a young woman whose rich attire proclaims her a companion or daughter of the house rather than a menial. The furnishings of the apartment are characterized by the unostentatious richness of Dutch luxury of the period. Through an open door in the rear of the room a glimpse is obtained of a sunlit garden. The coloring is ripe and strong, and the picture is held together by a fine harmony of tone. It fully justifies the high encomium passed on the artist by the distinguished French critic, and the exalted reputation which all Europe accorded the painter during his lifetime.

No. 216

JEAN BAPTISTE ANTOINE GUILLEMET....Paris

Born at Chantilly. · Pupil of Corot and of Oudinot. Medals,
1874, 1876. Chevalier of the Legion of Honor, 1880.

" Landscape "

14 X 22

" Guillemet is a painter who does not pursue chimeras.   He paints
nature in her grandeur, sincerely and with a religious horror of
exaggeration.   Well educated in the classics as a doctor of the
Sarbonne, one never hears him discourse in the affected jargon of
the studios.   He introduced himself to the illustrious Corot and enjoyed the benefit of his counsels.   Through Corot he made the
acquaintance of Barye, of Daumier and Vollon, who were his friends
and advisers.   In 1869 he profited by the wise hints of Courbet, and
his very debut, thanks to these advantages, was brilliant and noteworthy."—BELINA : *Nos Peintres,* 1883.

Although to a certain extent a pupil of Corot, Guillemet has been fortunate
in possessing an original strength of mind that preserved him from falling
slavishly into the master's tracks. The best of Corot, the quest for perfection of
tonality, he acquired and developed.   When, in one of his pictures, the tones
and values have fallen into their true relations, he considers the work complete
and sets it by without elaborating it with encumbering detail. One of the
first pictures he exhibited, " Bercy in December," was considered of such an
order of merit that the government acquired it for the Luxembourg collection,
in 1874, and in 1880 his artistic merit won for the artist the coveted decoration
of the Legion of Honor.

No. 217

WILLIAM FERON..........................Paris

Born at Stockholm, Sweden. Studied at the Academy of Fine Arts of Stockholm.

"Low Tide: Boulogne"

28 x 20

"With a soft, slow, gentle motion
  Swings the ebb tide to the sea;
  Swings the slow tide hushfully
To the distant, restless ocean."

—WILLIAM SHARP.

The fishing boats and the tide are out together. The long reaches of sand gleam wet and yellow in the summer sunlight. The brightness of a fair day flashes in ripples of reflected gold upon the treacherous sea. Ashore the old and feeble, the women and the babes alone are left, while all who can pull rope or handle oar are off to wrest a living from the deep. There is nothing uncommon in this desertion of a French fishing village by all its able-bodied denizens. Often, indeed, at certain seasons, the women too are away, and the chance traveller finds the cabins inhabited only by the blind or palsied grand-sire and the babe in its untended cradle. The fisher girl in this picture is for the present an idler. She has carried her knitting down to the shore, there to await the return of the boats which will bring back to her a lusty sweetheart and a task in helping him unload his finny spoil. The fair sky carries no threat of danger to her heart, and so she knits and sings in the sunlight, happy in the thought that he is safe to return to her when the day's work is done.

No. 218

THEODORE ROUSSEAU (deceased)

Born at Paris, 1812. Pupil of Lethiere. Showed himself a naturalist from the first, and for thirteen years was excluded from the Salon by an Academic jury. First exhibited in 1834. Medals, 1834, 1849, 1855. Chevalier of the Legion of Honor, 1852. One of the Eight Grand Medals of Honor (Exposition Universalle), Paris, 1867. Died, 1867. Diploma to the Memory of Deceased Artists, 1878.

" Twilight "

6 x 12

" He excelled Corot in combining with a thorough draughtsmanship a rich scheme of color. In 1857 Edmond About wrote : ' For twenty-five years Theodore Rousseau has been the first apostle of truth in landscape—above all, a colorist.' His genius transformed the commonest aspect of nature into a poem ; he could paint the storm as well as the smile of nature. He was intensely French, and to his love of landscape was added the love of his native land. He painted many pictures of sunrise and sunset, in which he illustrated the principle which he expressed in saying: ' Light spread over a work is universal life ; without light there is no creation.' "— STRANAHAN : "*History of French Painting.*"

There are no tenderer or more poetical productions of Rousseau's brush than his studies of the glory and the mystery of departing day. The enormous power of color that he possessed found in these subjects opportunities for a full display of itself, while his own mental bent was in harmony with the pensiveness and solemnity that attend the death of day. He gave to these pictures a dramatic—often even a tragic character; where in Corot they had the charm of dreaminess and peace. Theophile Thoré relates of him that he would arise at night from his troubled sleep, and by the uncertain light of a flickering lamp perpetuate on the canvas his memories of the splendor of an evening sky seen from his garret window, and made magnificent by the reflection of the dreams in which the picture of his mind had haunted him until it became a tangible thing. During the years he had spent at Barbizon, even the simple villagers learned to call an exceptionally splendid and colorful sunset a "Rousseau sky."

No. 219

N. A. BROOKS

"An Actual Necessity"

10 X 8

"Some alleged philosopher has stated that there is no really imperative necessity in life. I dispute this statement. I dispute it from foundation to apex. I am personally conversant of one absolute and peremptory necessity in human existence, a necessity that no man can escape from. It is money. You may call it what you will—pounds, shillings and pence, or dollars and cents—but it remains a fact that it is, beyond all dispute, to all people who have to live in this world, an inescapable, a tyrannical and an actual necessity."— ALBERT SMITH.

Mr. Brooks paints this necessity in simple shape—in the shape of a $5 note of current currency, to wit. He paints it, moreover, with an illusory power not at all common. There are a great many people who would try to pick up this bank-bill if they saw it on the floor, and be astonished to discover that it was the coinage of talent, instead of the mint. It is but an artful counterfeit, but, unlike most counterfeits, it may be said of this one that it is worth, in the open market, a great deal more than its original.

No. 220

FREDERICK SCHUCHARD............New York

Born in New York, 1855. Pupil of William Morgan and J. G. Brown.

" The Little Florist "

20 X 14

" In all places then, and in all seasons,
    Flowers expand their light and soul-like wings,
    Teaching us by most persuasive reasons
    How akin they are to human things.

" And with childlike, credulous affection
    We behold their tender buds expand ;
    Emblems of our own great resurrection,
    Emblems of the bright and better land."
           —H. W. LONGFELLOW : *"Flowers."*

The little florist of the artist has been experimenting in domestic floriculture. She has been pruning and trimming the potted plants of the household until she finds herself at a loss for further improvements upon them and is left, with ferns and blossoms, to fashion herself a bouquet. The lessons that the poet reads in the flowers have not yet reached her childish heart. What she finds in them to admire and wonder at is their beauty and fragrance and the mystery in which these qualities originate, problems which are, indeed, sufficient in themselves to puzzle wiser and maturer minds than that of a little maiden on a doorstep, playing at gardening with her lap full of trophies of her skill.

14 ?!!

www.ingramcontent.com/pod-product-compliance
Lightning Source LLC
Chambersburg PA
CBHW031443270326
41930CB00007B/854

9 7 8 3 7 4 4 6 5 7 3 5 8